Cambridge Elements ≡

Elements in Publishing and Book Culture
edited by
Samantha Rayner
University College London
Leah Tether
University of Bristol

THE NETWORK TURN

Changing Perspectives in the Humanities

Ruth Ahnert

Queen Mary University of London

Sebastian E. Ahnert

University of Cambridge

Catherine Nicole Coleman

Stanford University

Scott B. Weingart

Carnegie Mellon University

CAMBRIDGE
UNIVERSITY PRESS

CAMBRIDGE
UNIVERSITY PRESS

University Printing House, Cambridge CB2 8BS, United Kingdom

One Liberty Plaza, 20th Floor, New York, NY 10006, USA

477 Williamstown Road, Port Melbourne, VIC 3207, Australia

314–321, 3rd Floor, Plot 3, Splendor Forum, Jasola District Centre,
New Delhi – 110025, India

79 Anson Road, #06–04/06, Singapore 079906

Cambridge University Press is part of the University of Cambridge.

It furthers the University's mission by disseminating knowledge in the pursuit of
education, learning, and research at the highest international levels of excellence.

www.cambridge.org
Information on this title: www.cambridge.org/9781108791908
DOI: 10.1017/9781108866804

First published 2020

A catalogue record for this publication is available from the British Library.

ISBN 978-1-108-79190-8 Paperback
ISSN 2514-8524 (online)
ISSN 2514-8516 (print)

The Network Turn

Changing Perspectives in the Humanities

Elements in Publishing and Book Culture

DOI: 10.1017/9781108866804

First published online: December 2020

Ruth Ahnert

Queen Mary University of London

Sebastian E. Ahnert

University of Cambridge

Catherine Nicole Coleman

Stanford University

Scott B. Weingart

Carnegie Mellon University

Author for correspondence: Ruth Ahnert, r.r.ahnert@qmul.ac.uk

ABSTRACT: We live in a networked world. Online social networking platforms and the World Wide Web have changed how society thinks about connectivity. Because of the technological nature of such networks, their study has predominantly taken place within the domains of computer science and related scientific fields. But arts and humanities scholars are increasingly using the same kinds of visual and quantitative analysis to shed light on aspects of culture and society hitherto concealed. This Element contends that networks are a category of study that cuts across traditional academic barriers, uniting diverse disciplines through a shared understanding of complexity in our world. Moreover, we are at a moment in time when it is crucial that arts and humanities scholars join the critique of how large-scale network data and advanced network analysis are being harnessed for the purposes of power, surveillance, and commercial gain.

This title is also available as Open Access on Cambridge Core at
http://dx.doi.org/10.1017/9781108866804

KEYWORDS: network analysis, network visualisation, digital humanities,
interdisciplinarity, complexity

ISBNs:9781108791908 (PB), 9781108866804 (OC)
ISSNs: 2514-8524 (online), 2514-8516 (print)

Contents

Introduction

In the days following the 9/11 terror attack, an FBI agent visited the Whitney Museum of American Art to see Mark Lombardi's 1996 drawing 'BCCI-ICIC & FAB, 1972–91 (4th version)' (Figure 1) (Hobbs, 2003: 11–12, 95–8). The web-like image comprises a meticulously researched diagram of individuals and groups with ties to a money-laundering organisation that operated under the name of the Bank of Commerce and Credit International (BCCI), which included Osama bin Laden and others associated with al-Qaeda. As Lombardi himself described, BCCI 'was used not only by drug dealers and con men but also by the governments of the US, UK, Saudi Arabia and the Gulf Arab states to funnel support to Afghan guerrillas fighting Soviet occupation, to pay off friends and adversaries alike and conduct secret arms sales to Iran' (Lombardi, 2001). In other words, in black and red ink, Lombardi traced a terrorist network that reached the centres of government. He had grasped the power of the network perspective to reveal conspiracy, adapting graphical traditions associated with the study of social networks developed in the first half of the twentieth century. Tragically, the significance of his research would be uncovered only after his death: in early 2002, a year after the artist's suicide, the FBI's Operation Green Quest raided the offices of several Virginia-based Islamic charities whose Saudi funders, including Mahfouz and prominent Bush backers, featured in Lombardi's work (Goldstone, 2015).

Three years after Lombardi produced his artwork, Albert-László Barabási and Réka Albert published a scientific article entitled 'Emergence of Scaling in Random Networks' (Barabási & Albert, 1999). It argued that a wide variety of seemingly heterogeneous networks, such as power grids, social networks, and the World Wide Web, exhibit nearly identical distributions of connectivity, and it offered an elegant model that explained how these distributions might arise.[1] This particular distribution of connectivity was different from those most scientists expected at the time.[2] The significance of Barabási and Albert's findings was that they provided a compelling case for analysing seemingly disparate systems and kinds of data using the same mathematical models and

---

[1] For the debate around this thesis, see Broido and Clauset (2019) and Holme (2019).
[2] For an earlier precedent, see Price (1965).

Figure 1 Lombardi, Mark (1951–2000), 'BCCI-ICIC & FAB, 1972–91 (4th version)' from the series BCCI, ICIC & FAB, 1996–2000. Graphite and coloured pencil on paper. New York, Whitney Museum of American Art. © 2019. Digital image. Whitney Museum of American Art / Licensed by Scala.

tools. For this reason, their article is regarded as one of the founding publications of the interdisciplinary field of modern network science. The argument for the application of analytical tools across domains was extended in Barabási's best-selling book *Linked*, in which he argued that many challenges in our world, such as managing the spread of epidemics, fighting terrorism, and handling economic crises, can be cracked by understanding these systems as networks (Barabási, 2002). As such, networks appear in Barabási's study as a kind of Rosetta Stone. This message reached 70,000 readers and thus played a small part in the rise of the 'network' perspective in the modern consciousness following the new millennium.

Lombardi and Barabási's work is part of what we call the 'network turn'. This turn cannot be attributed to either the artist or the scientist; they are but two examples of a whole host of converging thoughts and practices around the turn of the new millennium – the zeitgeist of the networked age. The World Wide Web had become available to the public only in 1991, but by 2004, the web-based view of relations manifested itself in an entirely new kind of communication platform when 'TheFacebook' was launched. The subsequent proliferation of social networking platforms has profoundly shaped the way we understand connectivity in the world today.

Another key driver of the network turn, highlighted by the FBI's interest in Lombardi's work, is terrorist activity – both in terms of the perceived threat of terrorist networks, and in the new technologies available to security agencies to mitigate against them. Following 9/11, using data-gathering approaches very similar to Lombardi's combined with computational analysis, Valdis Krebs used public information and newspaper clippings to produce a partial map of the social network behind the attack. His network analysis showed that all nineteen of the hijackers were within two email or phone call connections of two al-Qaeda members already known to the CIA before the attack. According to three common network analysis metrics, the network's most central figure was Muhammed Atta, who turned out to be the ringleader (Krebs, 2001). Krebs' findings raised the important question of whether the attack could have been predicted. Shortly after posting his analysis online, Krebs was invited to Washington, DC to brief intelligence contractors. The extent to which Krebs' insight about the power of network analysis fed into the existing methods that intelligence agencies employed is hard to gauge, but by

2013, as the leak by Edward Snowden brought to light, the National Security Agency was engaged in massive-scale network analysis using data from nine internet providers.

The study and critique of networks has predominantly taken place within the domains of computer science and related scientific fields, the military, and the tech sector due to the scale of digital data being analysed and the nature of the investigations prompting their study. This book not only argues that arts and humanities scholars can use the same kind of visual and quantitative analysis of networks to shed light on the study of culture; it also contends that the critical skills native to humanistic inquiry are vital to the theorisation and critique of our networked world. Network analysis, as we define it in this book, is a set of practices and discourses that sit at the interface of the natural sciences, humanities, social sciences, computer science, and design. We contend that networks are a category of study that cuts across traditional academic boundaries and that has the potential to unite diverse disciplines through a shared understanding of complexity in our world – whether that complexity pertains to the nature of the interactions of proteins in gene-regulatory networks or to the network of textual variants that can reveal the lineage of a poem. Moreover, this shared framework provides a compelling case for collaboration across those boundaries, for bringing together computational tools for quantitative network analysis, together with theories, discourses, and applied techniques from the social sciences, the humanities, visual design, and art practice.

The cases of Lombardi and Barabási provide an instructive way of grasping that shared framework because, superficially, their work has very little in common. Barabási and Albert explicitly cite the computerisation of data acquisition as essential to their research. By contrast, Lombardi's research process was analogue. He gathered his data on three-by-five notecards. There is no evidence that Lombardi read Barabási and Albert's groundbreaking work in statistics and physics; rather, his inspiration was panorama and history painting. He used the term 'narrative structures' to describe his hand-drawn webs of connection. Produced through an iterative process of refinement, the work is human in scale, legible visually in its entirety. Perhaps more importantly, it is his interpretation of a carefully researched but inevitably incomplete record. It does not pretend to objectivity. In stark contrast, Barabási and Albert's method is scientific: it proposes a model to predict the behaviour of systems and to understand complex topologies 'independent of the system and the identity of its constituents' (Barabási & Albert, 1999). Thus, where Lombardi is analysing past events, Barabási and Albert offer a predictive model; where Lombardi is visual, Barabási and Albert use algorithms designed to detect patterns in data sets too large or complex for the human eye to detect. These approaches seem to occupy two very separate worlds.

Nevertheless, Lombardi's art and the scientific approaches of Barabási and Albert have much in common. Lombardi distils the composition of relationships in history painting and the comprehensive 'at one view' of the panorama into a formal abstraction rooted in the conceptual art movement of the mid-twentieth century, and reflects the overlapping concerns, discourses, and methods of art and science. The artist and scientists use connectivity to make sense out of data: a representation of knowledge that relies on abstraction. Both produce results that are seductive in their elegance and simplicity. Networks are by definition an abstraction into a system of nodes and edges. Nodes are entities; edges are the relationships between them. Two examples can be seen in Figure 2. Such an abstract system is inherently intuitive. These two elements, nodes and edges, are the simple building blocks of an obviously abbreviated rendering, a malleable geometry that can range in complexity from a direct and declarative schematic to a dense, indecipherable web of connections.

The worlds from which the artist and the scientists emerge have their own long genealogies. The standard history we tell for network science traces its lineage back through graph theory to Leonard Euler's solution of the Königsberg Bridge problem in 1736. Similarly, we might argue that artists and humanities scholars have been engaging with network-analytic approaches for at least sixty years. However, these threads have visibly come together only in the past twenty years. In the first decade following the millennium, some pioneers began to apply the methods of network science to the study of cultural artefacts, but most scholars were still learning how to query web-based digitised archives without attention to the computer networks invisibly underpinning this virtual archival experience. However, since 2010 there has been a slow but steady increase in scholars in the arts and humanities employing network visualisation, social

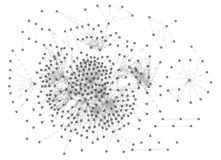

Figure 2 Networks consist of nodes and edges. On the left, a simple network of six nodes and seven edges. On the right, a more complex network (with several disjointed components) that depicts social relationships in a Protestant underground community during the reign of Queen Mary I of England (see Ahnert & Ahnert, 2015). Diagram by the authors.

network analysis theory, and quantitative measures from network science to address their research questions. In addition to a rise in the number of publications invoking these methodologies, the clear demand for work-shops and training in network visualisation and analysis tailored to arts and humanities scholars is evidence of these approaches gaining traction. Such work still tends to be a fringe activity, though, and suspicion among more traditional elements within the disciplines who have interpreted the computational tools and methods associated with network analysis as part of the incursion of scientific method into their domain, which has sometimes been conflated with the neoliberal takeover of the university.

This book does not call for arts and humanities scholars to accept unquestioningly frameworks and methods developed in the field of network science. Rather, it argues that the discourse and analysis of networks can move forward only through collaboration and exchange at the interface of computational method, humanistic inquiry, and design practice. The case for scholars from the arts and humanities engaging with networks is compelling on a number of levels. The use of computational network analysis can lead to the creation of new knowledge, and to the corroboration of theories. It makes it possible, with relative ease and speed, to measure the relationships between many entities in multiple ways, allowing a rich, multidimensional reading of complex systems never possible before. It has proven to be an effective tool for understanding metric data on a very large scale. A seemingly infinite number of calculations can be run on the resulting network to filter and parse that large-scale data, giving a more nuanced understanding of both the local and the global. The ability to analyse data across scales has been rendered increasingly necessary in light of the ever-growing quantity of information made available through the digitisation of our cultural artefacts. Networks further offer the ability to contextualise the large scale with the small and vice versa, breaking the explanatory chasm between part and whole.

Moreover, scholars from the arts and humanities already have the conceptual framework to make this leap: they have been writing about networks for centuries, albeit from the metaphorical perspective, examining communities of practitioners, the dissemination of ideas, or the relationships between certain texts, images, or artefacts. Although researchers with standard humanities training will likely need to acquire some new skills to engage with the computational challenges of network visualisation and quantitative analysis, we contend that they already have a set of skills that are key to the development of the interdisciplinary practice of network analysis. This is not just about receiving wholesale methods and theories developed in the computational and social sciences; rather, the critical skills developed in the arts and humanities are needed to complicate and nuance the current ways in which data are collected, modelled, and queried in the field of network science. Finally, we are at a moment in time when it is crucial that arts and humanities scholars engage critically with both the potential and the pitfalls of technological advancements. By offering an understanding of how networks work, we provide a much-needed framework to articulate how companies and governments can exploit the harnessing of large-scale data and advanced network analysis for the purposes of power, surveillance, and commercial gain.

This book is not a how-to manual: it does not provide instruction in the basics of network analysis or the use of 'out-of-the-box' tools, or an introduction to programming, as a plethora of other resources already do this.[3] Our aim here is more ideological. We seek to open up a space for exchange between the humanities, arts, and sciences – a space that is genuinely collaborative, that is mutually beneficial, and that recognises that networks present a mode of inquiry that draws on knowledge and practices from all these domains. Its combined brevity and breadth mean that it is not the final word, but rather a provocation. We hope this book will be a starting point for debate: not just in the digital humanities community (who are already used to situating themselves at the intersections of disciplines), and not just in the arts and humanities, but also in the natural, social, and computer sciences. It is the desire to engage and debate that motivated us to offer this book open access. Our most basic aim is to persuade colleagues in the arts and humanities of the value of networks as a conceptual and methodological framework that supplements (but does not replace) traditional methods of inquiry. But our intentions are broader than that: we hope for a sharing across domains to deepen our understanding of networks. That deepening is gained by combining world views we might attribute on one hand to Lombardi and on the other to Barabási, the combination of careful research and a choice of parameters at the human scale, that is not only coupled with but iteratively developed in tandem with the power of computational analysis.

Part of the argument for multiple perspectives is manifested in the way this book has been written. It is the product of a collaboration between a scholar of English literature, book history, and digital methods, a physicist specialising in network science, a historian of science concentrating in digital humanities, and a digital research architect with a background in design and tool development. We have not split the chapters among different authors; rather the arguments are the product of ongoing debate among the four of us over a period of three and a half years. Such a process of creation, like much of the work going on within network analysis more broadly, necessitates co-authorship. This is something that remains relatively rare in the arts and humanities. We seek to demonstrate the benefits of co-authorship, the insights and perspectives it brings, which can rarely be replicated by a single-authored work. It is not a shortcut or a faster route to publication. The process of gaining understanding,

---

[3] For a useful overview of tools and tutorials, see http://historicalnetworkresearch. org/resources/external-resources/.

compromising, and iterating our arguments necessarily takes longer than writing a piece from a single viewpoint. However, we believe that process makes the work stronger. Genuine, deep sharing of ideas across disciplinary boundaries takes patience, goodwill, and a desire to learn and be challenged. We are therefore not simply arguing for a set of methodologies and discourses associated with the network framework. The network turn brings with it a set of research and publication practices that are inherently collaborative and dialogic.

The six chapters that follow are organised into three parts. Part I offers 'Frameworks' for understanding the methods developed in the natural, computational, and social sciences. To fully harness the analytical power of networks, we must first attend to the way a specific set of Western linguistic, disciplinary, and visual histories of networks frame the systems and phenomena we observe in the world, shaping, limiting, opening, and reorienting the questions we ask. Part II introduces 'Cultural Networks', giving an overview of the ways in which networks have already been used to examine cultural phenomena and artefacts, and the important role of design principles in both querying our data and communicating our research. Finally, Part III examines how network analysis provides a set of 'Manoeuvres': intellectual manoeuvres that refigure cultural objects in our minds as abstract systems of nodes and edges, mechanical manoeuvres that structure data and navigate input versus output, and manoeuvres between a landscape of abstraction and research questions that are steeped in contextual information. Taken together, these processes seek to dismantle the binaries between the 'humanistic' and the 'scientific' and, in so doing, create new norms of practice and inquiry. These new norms, however, are yet to be established. They must necessarily be shaped in ongoing collaboration and exchange. In the closing pages, we therefore suggest how different groups of scholars, practitioners, and professionals can direct the network turn as it becomes a standard part of our critical cultural apparatus.

Part I Frameworks

Networks represent more than a scientific method; they are a mindset shaped by a rich conceptual and visual history. To fully harness the analytical power of networks, we must first attend to the way these histories frame observable systems and phenomena in the world, shaping, limiting, opening, and reorienting the questions we ask.

1 Networks Are Always Metaphorical

In network science, researchers utilise networks as a formalised abstraction that permits computational analysis. In the humanities, by comparison, scholars largely employ networks as a metaphor. Despite these methodological differences, there are important continuities between the act of abstraction and use of metaphor. George Lakoff and Mark Johnson argue that metaphors are not just linguistic embellishment, but rather provide a conceptual framework that structures our most basic understandings of the world (Lakoff & Johnson, 1980). Lakoff and Raphael Núñez later applied the framework of conceptual metaphor to the domain of mathematics:

> Conceptual metaphor is a cognitive mechanism for allowing us to reason about one kind of thing as if it were another ... It is a grounded, inference-preserving cross-domain mapping – a neural mechanism that allows us to use the inferential structure of one conceptual domain (say, geometry) to reason about another (say, arithmetic). (Lakoff & Núñez, 2000: 6)

This is precisely how networks are used in the sciences. To the scientist a network is an abstract object, a collection of pairwise relationships (termed 'edges', 'links', or 'arcs') between defined entities (termed 'nodes' or 'vertices'). What receives surprisingly little attention in scientific network literature is the definition of those entities and relationships, or, in other words, the process of abstraction from the real world to the network representation. Network science as a field takes the abstract network as a starting point; the process of abstraction often belongs to another domain, namely that in which the network data originates. A historical correspondence network originates in the domain of history, a network of neurons in the domain of neuroscience. Because the process of abstraction leads us across disciplinary boundaries, both the original domain and network science often neglect it. To see the network as a metaphor, by contrast, we have to be fully aware of the process of abstraction: what information it prioritises and what the abstraction elides.

This chapter argues that researchers who employ networks as a metaphor (traditionally those in the arts and humanities) ought to be familiar with the mathematical formalisations. Conversely, scholars wedded to the computational power of quantitative network analysis should be aware that its power derives from its reliance on the metaphorical dimension and an act of interpretation. For this reason we sketch the Western cultural history of the network as a concept, tracing its etymology and its acceptance as an inferential structure that enables interrogation and discovery. Undertaking such a task, which spans centuries as well as disciplines, in just a handful of pages means that the resulting account is also necessarily an abstraction. Moreover, it relies on readily available sources such as the *Oxford English Dictionary* (*OED*) and the Google Books corpus, which bring with them their own set of biases – not least an anglophone focus. However, even with the partiality and brevity of our rendering, the shifting applications of the word 'network' chart a series of changing views on the organisation of our world and how we can begin to understand it.

Importantly, taking such an approach removes the narrative of novelty from networks. It is easy to think of the network as a modern concept, and it is certainly the impression we take away if we rely solely on the snapshot of the word's usage provided by Google Ngrams (see Figure 3). The Ngram shows limited usage in the nineteenth century, an upward curve beginning around 1920, and a sharp uptick after 1980; only isolated references occur before. However, the problems of the Google Books corpus for nuanced linguistic analysis are by now well documented, including the impact of optical character recognition (OCR) errors, the over-representation of scientific literature, messy metadata, the equal weight assigned to each book regardless of its literary impact, and the compounded bias of aggregated source libraries (Pechenick, Danforth, & Dodds, 2015). The latter means that a single, prolific author can noticeably insert new phrases into the Google Books lexicon, whether the author is widely read or not.

A complementary view is provided by the *OED* which lets us see some isolated data points from before 1800 in context. The earliest cited usage is in William Tyndale's 1530 translation of the Pentateuch: 'And he made a brasen gredyren of networke' (*OED*, 'network', n. 1.a). In this context the words describe a physical work, a gridiron ('gredyren'), which is constructed from

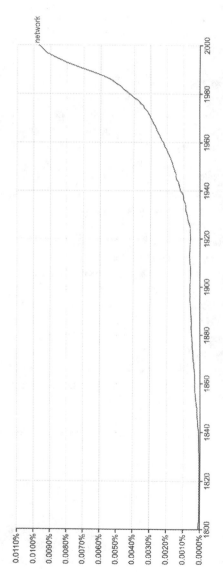

Figure 3 Frequency of the word 'network' in the English Google Books corpus between 1800 and 2000, generated using the Google Ngrams tool, with smoothing parameter set to 3.

parallel bars, crossed or interlaced in the fashion of a net. Mail armour was formed as a network, and the term was also used to describe fabric during the early modern period. The component words, 'net' and 'work', are from common Germanic stock; the composite, however, seems to be an English coinage, although it has made its way into numerous languages including Danish (*netværk*), Dutch (*netwerk*), German (*Netzwerk*), Maltese (*netwerk*), Norwegian (*nettverk*), and Swedish (*nätverk*). The word for network in certain other languages carries the same lineage from the word for the material act of weaving nets. For example, the Italian for network is *rete*, which comes from the Latin *rete*, meaning 'net' (the same root as *red* in Spanish, *rede* in Portuguese and Galician, and *rețea* in Romanian). In English, the root 'ret' forms the basis of 'reticulation' (a pattern of interlacing lines) and 'retina' (the regular net-like arrangement of blood vessels in the eye). The etymology of 'network' in both Germanic and Romance languages, therefore, contains a set of assumptions about structure, pattern, order, and distribution. In many cases, a maker or designer is implied.

It is important to recognise these assumptions when we communicate across disciplinary boundaries because the kinds of complex systems the word 'network' is now more often used to describe do not necessarily share the ordered woven structural features of mail armour or gridirons. In the modern language of networks, these particular material forms might be referred to instead as *lattices*, a specific subcategory of networks. The development of the word 'network' as a metaphor for systems that have very different patterns of distribution from fabric or mail armour can be seen from at least the seventeenth century, when it was used to describe the system of arteries, veins, and capillaries in humans and animals – what we might describe as rhizomatic structures. Later, as people recognised these patterns in both natural and artificial systems, the word 'network' came to represent systems of interconnection in general.

The evolution of the concept to denote the physical infrastructures for the distribution of people, merchandise, and electricity to consumers follows the construction of those systems relatively swiftly. For example, the first purpose-built passenger railway, the Liverpool and Manchester Railway, was authorised by an Act of Parliament in 1826, and by 1836 nearly 400 miles of track had opened in England. During this period, competition emerged regarding different scales of gauge, in response to which Thornton Hunt published a tract in 1846 entitled *Unity of the Iron Network; Showing How the Last Argument for the Break of Gauge, Competition, Is at Variance with the True Interests of the Public.* 'Iron network' might be described as an allusive rather than descriptive metaphor (e.g. railway network). The decision to use this as the main title therefore suggests that the metaphor was already an established way of describing the rail system. Similarly, the idea of investing in a central plant and network to deliver electricity to customers was first acted upon in the late 1870s, and by 1883 references appear in technical journal articles to networks of conductors in the construction of street mains electricity (*OED*, 'network', n. 4.b.).

In the twentieth century, we see the emergence of domain-specific appropriations of the word, which happened in tandem with a long philosophical and cultural crisis surrounding the rise of secular and democratic societies. The 1934 book *Who Shall Survive?* that emerged from the research undertaken by Jacob Moreno and Helen Hall Jennings contains some of the earliest graphical depictions of social networks, known as sociograms (see Figure 4).[4] Moreno and Jennings were founders of the journal *Sociometry*, which was the venue for some of the earliest scholarly articles in this new field. Moreno and Jennings claimed that 'before the advent of sociometry no one knew what the interpersonal structure of a group "precisely" looked like' (Moreno [& Jennings], 1953: lvi). The sociogram can be seen as the precursor both to the graphical notation employed by the artist Mark Lombardi, and the network visualisation layouts now familiar to us thanks to the ubiquity of out-of-the-box tools like Gephi (discussed further in Chapter 4). For most of the remainder of the twentieth century, social network analysis followed in the footsteps of Moreno and Jennings, collecting small-scale social networks through intensive surveys of well-defined social groups, numbering typically fewer than 100 individuals, which can be rendered intuitively using the sociogram.

Social network analysis also produced a number of concepts and measurements that have crucially changed the metaphorical hinterland of the

---

[4] Moreno was listed as the sole author of this book, although Jennings was credited with the authorship of a 'supplement'. Nonetheless, his acknowledgements do include the phrase 'I and my collaborator, Helen Jennings'. Linton Freeman contends that the completed research and the publications drew heavily on Jennings' contributions (Freeman, 2004: 35–6).

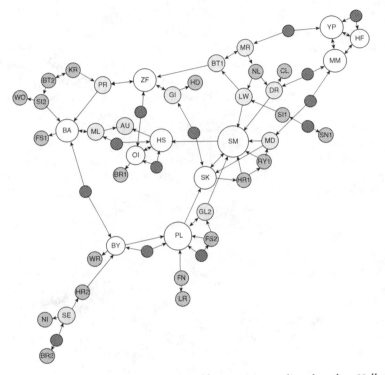

Figure 4 Redesigned network produced by Martin Grandjean based on Hall and Moreno's work in *Who Shall Survive?* showing relationships between children in a classroom (Grandjean, 2015, chosen due to original diagrams being in copyright). CC BY SA 4.0.

word 'network'. Central to this changing conceptual framework was the discovery that in social networks, two people are, on average, only separated by a small number of steps. In 1929, the popular Hungarian author Frigyes Karinthy wrote 'Láncszemek' ('Chain-Links'), a short story musing on the shrinking social world during a period of rich international trade in Hungary. In the novel, Karinthy's characters create a game:

One of us suggested performing the following experiment to prove that the population of the Earth is closer together now than they have ever been before. We should select any person from the 1.5 billion inhabitants of the Earth – anyone, anywhere at all. He bet us that, using no more than *five* individuals, one of whom is a personal acquaintance, he could contact the selected individual using nothing except the network of personal acquaintances. (Karinthy, 1929)

Karinthy's game became reality in Stanley Milgram's research into the 'small world' phenomenon just over three decades later. Building on his earlier work with the mathematician Manfred Kochen and the political scientist Ithiel de Sola Pool, Milgram undertook a series of experiments that sought to determine the degrees of separation between people in real-world networks, which he reported in a 1967 issue of the popular magazine *Psychology Today*. Milgram invited members of the public to forward a parcel to close acquaintances in their immediate social (but not necessarily geographical) neighbourhood with the goal of eventually reaching a particular individual on the other side of the country. Although the methods and findings have since been disputed, Milgram claimed his study showed that 'only five intermediaries will, on average, suffice to link any two randomly chosen individuals, no matter where they happen to live in the United States' (Milgram, 1967: 66). Milgram's article generated enormous publicity, thereby connecting in a public consciousness the concept of the network and that of the small world.[5] More recently the findings have been popularised as the theory of 'six degrees of separation'. Conceptually this phrase makes sense only if you view the world in terms of the network. The network, then, is a pre-existing framework upon which the concept of six degrees of separation is drawn.

Interestingly, while the phrase is usually attributed to Milgram, it is more likely that John Guare popularised it through his 1990 play *Six Degrees of Separation*, which spawned a film of the same name in 1993.

---

[5] Milgram's experiments, it is now known, were plagued by high non-completion rates (Watts, 2004: 133–40).

What is helpful about approaching the sociological findings of Milgram's experiments via this play is that it captures the surprise Milgram's discoveries generated and what they might mean for lived experience. The character Ouisa Kittredge says:

> I read somewhere that everybody on this planet is separated by only six other people. Six degrees of separation. Between us and everybody else on this planet. The president of the United States. A gondolier in Venice. Fill in the names. I find that A) tremendously comforting that we're so close and B) like Chinese water torture that we're so close. Because you have to find the right six people to make the connection. It's not just big names. It's anyone. A native in a rain forest. A Tierra del Fuegan. An Eskimo. I am bound to everyone on this planet by a trail of six people. (Guare, 1990: 81)

The accessibility of the concept of six degrees of separation is shown by the way it has been seized on in popular culture. The parlour game 'Six degrees of Kevin Bacon' challenges players to find the shortest path between a given actor or actress and prolific actor Kevin Bacon (which is in turn referenced by the digital project Six Degrees of Francis Bacon). And the phrase has appeared as a title of two TV series (a drama about six New Yorkers, *Six Degrees*, and a comedy reality show, *Six Degrees of Everything*), songs by the bands Scouting for Girls and The Script and by country artist Miranda Lambert, and an episode in *Battlestar Galactica*. What is notable about Guare's monologue, and what seems to make the concept so appealing, is the invisibility of the connections, the difficulty of discovering them, and the sense of wonderment when they emerge.

That sense of wonder, however, is arguably a residue of the analogue era. By contrast, from the late 1990s onwards the rapid growth of both the Internet and computational processing power has made it possible to gather and analyse network data on an unprecedented scale. Now in a few lines of code we can construct and measure networks of various kinds and extract information about their global structure: how big they were, how densely clustered, and in the case of the small world phenomenon, how many degrees on average any randomly selected node was from any other node in a network. In the foundational 1998 publication 'Collective Dynamics of Small World Networks', Duncan J. Watts and Steven Strogatz showed how small world properties are not limited to social networks: the neural network of the worm *Caenorhabditis elegans*, the power grid of the western United States, and the collaboration graph of film actors are all small world networks (Watts & Strogatz, 1998). Together with the 1999 publication by Albert-László Barabási and Réka Albert discussed in the opening pages of this book, Watts and Strogatz's publication ushered in the field of network science. Whilst some of their observations had precedents in scientific scholarship, they shone light on the elegance of networks as an abstract framework, which opened the floodgates to natural scientists, computer scientists, and applied mathematicians working on network data.

The movement into the digital realm, however, does something to the way we think about networks. It seems to make scientists custodians of the knowledge we have about networks, even though the systems they are analysing are historically the intellectual domains of very different disciplines. By thinking of them as something that can be measured mathematically, they no longer seem metaphorical but real and knowable. However, science is not the saviour of these other disciplines; rather, these discoveries depend on the convergence of numerous disciplines that have zeroed in on one way of understanding the world. In the potted history outlined earlier, we see that the understanding of and public access to the concept of small world networks was shaped by novelists (Karinthy), mathematicians (Kochen, Strogatz), political scientists (de Sola Pool), social psychologists (Milgram), playwrights (Guare), sociologists (Watts), artists and archivists (Lombardi), and physicists (Barabási, Albert), amongst others. The network turn is a product of all of this work, and all of this work was fertilised in a world increasingly straining against its hierarchies of power amidst renewed pushes for decentralised infrastructures of transportation and communication.

However, among these many diverse disciplinary threads that converge in the network turn, the mathematical view is particularly amplified in the digital context, meaning that the metaphorical and human-scale issues of point of view, uncertainty, and exclusion have been sidelined in both the popular and the academic consciousness. We need to redirect attention to the metaphorical dimension because of the way it helps us pay attention to the role of human interpretation: the insights the metaphor provides also necessarily impose constraints on thinking. We must recognise how the etymological root of the word continues to shape research into the network phenomenon. When we employ the word 'network' now, we no longer think of physical woven nets or the regular lattice pattern it signified in the earliest known uses; yet the underlying assumption of systematic pattern still pertains to the extent that academic research into networks is still bound up with the task of accounting for those perceived patterns. One might argue that the way networks are imagined is irrelevant to their quantitative measurements, but ultimately such measures are always interpreted in terms of their meaning for the underlying network. And this interpretation is inextricably connected to our imagination of the network.

One of the main reasons Barabási's and Albert's 1999 paper became so foundational is because it confounded widespread assumptions regarding the connectivity of large real-world networks. Before information and communications technology made it possible to gather and analyse large-scale network data in the 1990s, such networks were often assumed to be simple random networks in which links exist with uniform probability. Barabási and Albert discovered that many real-world networks have a very different connectivity – one in which a small number of nodes are very highly connected, a larger number of nodes are reasonably well connected, and the vast majority are poorly connected. Moreover this distribution holds across different scales, making it *scale-free*. This means that in any specific region of the network, regardless of its size, we will also see a small number of relatively well-connected nodes and a large number of poorly connected nodes. Although the word 'network' no longer so strongly connotes the regularity it once implied, post-Barabási network science nonetheless operates on the foundation that physical, social, and biological networks are united by regularities in structure and form which allow for a combined science of networks that transcends traditional disciplines. Regularity is a thread still woven deeply into the fabric of networks.

Network measurements are also often conceived with a particular imagined network topology or visual paradigm in mind, and their quantitative rigour cannot entirely free them from this. The popularity of graph drawings to represent social relationships preceded measurements that focused on features like path and centrality. A 'community' in such drawings is most often defined as a network region that is more densely connected internally than it is to other network regions. Articles on these methods often feature artificial networks as test cases which have clusters of nodes with high internal connection density and few connections between them. As the field has discovered in the years since such methods were first devised, real-world network communities often do not match this simple imagined community structure. It has been shown that the dozens of different algorithms that grapple with the problem of defining and identifying varying notions of communities in fact demonstrate the *shortcomings* of the idea of defining network communities in the first place.

The metaphorical dimension of the network allows network scientists to imagine possible ways of navigating mathematical spaces that are both conceptually and topologically vast. The lens of metaphor, therefore, could be described as limiting, but this limitation is productive, giving researchers somewhere to begin their explorations. However, the moment we have identified as the network turn, around the new millennium, has yet to be self-reflexively theorised in this way, and as such the ways this metaphorical framework can be harnessed and challenged remain unexplored. In this gap lies an open invitation for arts and humanities scholars to add their expertise.

Moreover, by recognising that the quantitative approaches leveraged in network science rely on thinking we normally associate with humanistic inquiry, we can begin to break down the barriers between the two cultures of sciences and humanities identified in C. P. Snow's 1959 Rede lecture. This recognition undercuts the perception of a one-way movement of methods and theories that have been developed and tested in the sciences to solve problems in the arts and humanities. Rather, the interface between these two traditionally divided kingdoms allows greater self-reflexivity about the extent to which networks are what Lakoff and Núñez describe as 'a cognitive mechanism' that crosses conceptual domains. However, whereas Lakoff and Núñez see a one-to-one mapping in the most basic description of conceptual metaphors, networks cross multiple domains: from the material domain (of literal net-making), to the linguistic and literary domain (of words used to conjure a sense of complex systems of entanglement), to the graphical or visual sphere (of technical or medical diagrams and of graphics designed for navigating transport systems), to the abstract realm (of nodes and edges measured in mathematical space). Apart from the literal act of net-making, all other renderings of the network leverage at least one of these other domains to make sense of their own. This suggests that networks are inherently domain-crossing. However, although a small but consistent stream of historians have been engaging in interdisciplinary network analysis since at least the 1960s, relatively few arts and humanities scholars are currently involved in this cross-disciplinary exchange and collaboration. We must address this weakness if the field is to become self-critical.

2 Historical Threads

But why would scholars from the arts and humanities bother themselves with the task of theorising and operating within this network turn? Just because we can challenge the divisions between intellectual and conceptual domains with network thinking, it does not follow that we should.

Perhaps our motivation to think through networks should be that it allows us to see features in history, language, literature, or art that would otherwise remain inscrutable. Perhaps we yearn for the ability to recognise patterns across disparate domains as simply kaleidoscoped manifestations of the startlingly predictable human condition. Perhaps the seamless connection between part and whole, the ability to connect the microhistory with the longue durée, explains the allure of this siren's song. These features certainly drew the natural and social sciences to the network turn, and the move has proven successful many times over. But humanistic incentives often differ from those guiding the sciences. Humanities scholars may seek network thinking for its ability to cut through hierarchies, allowing us to draw threads between and through the geopolitical hegemonies that are often reflected in the construction of physical archives. Networks might give us the language to speak truth to power in configurations learned from and reminiscent of the US civil rights movement, the Iranian Green Movement, or the Extinction Rebellion. The network turn has this capacity as well, and we discuss many of these beneficial network affordances in subsequent chapters.

There are many principled reasons for scholars to engage with networks, but we suspect these are not the reasons the network turn is gripping the humanities, the sciences, and the larger world. Instead, a thousand years of self-reinforcing cultural, technological, and cognitive trends conspired to make the network turn inescapable. We are entangled in a web of fibre optic threads across which political revolutionaries, authoritarian surveillance states, ad-driven technocracies, populist politicians, and chaotic hacker collectives vie for control. The network turn has become complicit in various hegemonic power structures. As centres of power take networks and network theory increasingly seriously, they build ever more network assumptions into their systems. This creates a positive feedback loop forcing much of the world into a network framework even when those structures make little sense (see Healy, 2015). We engage with networks not because it would be *irresponsible* not to, true though that might be, but because it becomes increasingly *impossible* not to.

And to understand how networks have actively structured a perception of the world, we must understand them within a millennium-long history of visual practices for depicting and grasping knowledge systems throughout Western Europe. The following chapter explores the epistemological repercussions of the shift from tree to network as the dominant visual system for charting systems of knowledge and information. By visualising knowledge itself as a tree, medieval thinkers ensured their intellectual descendants would think of concepts as part of hierarchies for hundreds of years. As colonial Europeans drifted away from strictly tree-based representations of knowledge, partially in response to engagement with classification systems outside of their own traditions, they also moved away from the sense that knowledge forms an absolute hierarchy. Many of the descendants of that philosophical school now see knowledge as a diffuse system of sparsely interconnected parts.

The genealogy we outline here is not a narrative of progress, revealing how in moving away from arboreal systems we gained a more 'true' sense of the world. Rather, we show how shifting metaphors for knowledge have shaped and reflected the way we think, and how this process has radically upended ideas of natural hierarchy and unity. This chapter therefore extends the discourse on conceptual metaphor from the previous chapter, exposing the deep link between visual culture and the network turn, and what it means for the way we think.

In this effort, we do not present a history in the traditional sense. Neither do we escape a necessary presentism. As many threads have woven together to spur the network turn, pulling those threads often leads us to similar but unrelated moments in our cultural past. What we present next, then, might be described using the rhizome metaphor of Felix Guattari and Gilles Deleuze's 1980 book *A Thousand Plateaus*, which the authors proffer as an alternative to the arborescent conception of knowledge. The rhizome is a subterranean plant stem that grows horizontally, sending out roots and shoots from its nodes, and was appropriated by Guattari and Deleuze to describe a model of knowledge that allows for multiple, non-hierarchical entry and exit points in data representation and interpretation. The following pages might be described as a select gathering of such shoots used to gesture towards the complex network of roots that contextualise the network turn, revealing a deep relationship between diagrams, ontologies, and epistemologies. How precisely these threads interweave is in urgent need of a longer and more sophisticated approach, and we leave this chapter here as a provocation to whomever finally writes that fuller history.

The first important relationship to understand is that between what we see and what we know. Our understanding and our illustrations of the world have always been entwined, and both have set the stage for the network turn. Aristotle wrote in *De Memoria et Reminiscentia* that 'it is impossible to think without an image, for the same phenomenon occurs in thinking as is found in the construction of geometrical figures' (quoted in Squire & Elsner, 2016). To many ancient Greek philosophers, words and language derive from inner images and knowledge always involves a visual object. The image–thought connection percolated through Christian teachings via St Augustine and his contemporaries and remained prominent until surprisingly recently.

Many prevailing thinkers of the early Middle Ages did not differentiate the order of knowledge from the order of being. An imaginative representation of a concept could therefore not be untangled from the concept itself. The trees of knowledge that scribes illustrated in their manuscripts and that later appeared in printed books, as in Figure 5, were not merely helpful organisational schemes, but indicative of real underlying connections between the branching concepts they depicted.

Visualisations help us to construct the objects of scientific study. When discussing microscopic observations of bacteria, the early twentieth-century scientist Ludwik Fleck noted that novices see only blobs when looking under the microscope, whereas with training, the expert finally discerns bacteria. With that training, however, the expert loses the ability to see anything that contradicts the form she knows to be visible. On this topic Lorraine Daston writes: 'Perception furnishes the universe. It doesn't create the universe, but it does shape and sort, outlining sharp edges and arranging parts into wholes' (Daston, 2008: 98). Thus cloud atlases and diagrams of rock strata become as prescriptive as they are descriptive, giving shape to the world around them. Scientific perception of objects is a deeply psychological affair. But physical objects are not the only entities susceptible to construction and shaping through their visual

Figure 5 Ramon Llull showing the *Arbor elementalis* to a monk in *Arbor scientiae* ([F. Fradin?],[1515]). Digital image. The Wellcome Collection. CC BY 4.0.

representation. More abstract visualisations, such as trees of knowledge, are equally capable of shaping our thoughts. Medieval scholars associated with *ars memoriae* ('the art of memory') believed their diagrams structurally reflected their world. They were partially right: our diagrams construct our world as much as they reflect it. The implication is that when we collectively settle on particular visual metaphors to order our world – like trees of knowledge – that representation radiates outward, shaping our thoughts in unexpected ways. Conversely and recursively, our understanding of our world shapes our visual metaphors. Many of the examples that follow reflect this observation.

Take, for example, the relationship between knowledge and trees, connected at least since the writing of Genesis. Although historical linguists do not trace a common lineage to either concept, the fact that 'truth' and 'tree' were both once *trēow*, and 'wit' (as in wisdom) and 'wood' (as in forest) were both once quite close to *vid* has inspired at least a thousand years' worth of puns (Larrington, 2008). We link the two concepts without a second thought, as when we look for the *root* of the problem or discuss *branches* of knowledge. This coincidental etymological overlap is perhaps indicative of the strangely linked stories of networks and disciplines. Throughout medieval Europe, and pushing well into the nineteenth century, knowledge and trees coincide frequently.

The earliest such trees to be widely replicated were representations of Aristotle's classification of categories, based on a third-century treatise by Porphyry. He split the Aristotelian system of categories into a series of branching dichotomies, using the metaphor of a tree. By the tenth century, a Latin translation by Boethius illustrated Porphyry's metaphorical tree as a visual one. By the twelfth century, this style of diagram had achieved widespread legibility as a visual metaphor to connect hierarchies, lineages, and orders (see Kruja et al., 2002; Drucker, 2014). Although other styles of diagrams of knowledge did exist, few if any were entirely free of implicit hierarchy. Ramon Llull's thirteenth-century *Arbor scientiae* is likely the first work that attempted to systematically represent all branches of knowledge on trees (see Figure 5). The treatise features sixteen illustrations, the first of which is a single tree of knowledge used as a sort of table of contents, with each of the following trees representing a single branch from the first.

Many of the visual aspects of these trees were reflected in and reinforced the philosophies of their times. Like contemporary genealogical trees, many of the earliest diagrams of knowledge placed the root at the top of the page, indicating at once closeness to divinity, temporal precedence, and hierarchical pre-eminence. As diagrams of both knowledge and genealogy began flipping 180 degrees between the twelfth and sixteenth centuries, that tight coupling between divinity, time, and pre-eminence also began to separate. Similarly, many hierarchical diagrams of knowledge used visual cues, like an encircling chain in Christophe de Savigny's sixteenth-century *Tableaux accomplis de tous les arts libéraux*, to bound knowledge and imply its completeness (see Figure 6). As the concepts of boundedness and completeness were challenged, so too were their visual representations.

One exemplar of these and other changes is visible in Francis Bacon's 1605 *The Advancement of Learning: On the Partitions of the Sciences*. In it, Bacon wrote: 'The Partition of Sciences are not like several lines that meet in one angle; but rather like branches of trees that meet in one stemme, which stemme for some dimension and space is entire and continued, before it break, and part it selfe into armes and boughes' (Bacon, 1640: 132). The highly influential book broke from predecessors in its challenge to the 'one root' model of knowledge, and in its shift of learning from a closed system to an open system capable of growth and change. Even as theologists and natural philosophers were starting to explicitly question the suitability of the tree as an ordering metaphor, however, the same thinkers often fell back on arboreal diagrams, linguistic metaphors, and the philosophical implications they entailed because that was simply the ontological architecture in which they had learned to think (Ariew, 1992).

While trees of knowledge continued to flourish in the seventeenth and eighteenth centuries, being used frequently as organisation schemes for libraries and booksellers' catalogues all across Europe, educators and natural philosophers increasingly questioned the ability of the tree to truly represent the world of knowledge. By 1759, the encyclopaedists Diderot and d'Alembert rejected even the idea of a proper order of knowledge. They introduced their *Encyclopedie* saying that unified orders of knowledge are essentially arbitrary and that there are as many different possible systems as there are projections of the world map (Ariew, 1992). Not only was there no such thing as a natural order to knowledge, there could not even be a proper genealogical order to knowledge. The editors were careful to separate those two concepts. In rejecting the definitive order of knowledge, however, the encyclopaedists faced a dilemma: their great project still needed to be organised in some fashion. And so, despite their misgivings, they introduced their work with a diagram of a tree.

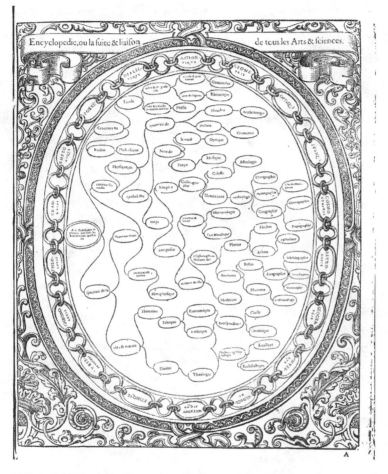

Figure 6 Christophe de Savigny's diagram partitioning the arts and sciences, in *Tableaux accomplis* (Gourmont, 1587). Digital image. Gallica, Bibliothèque nationale de France. Public domain.

The tree of knowledge was killed and revived frequently throughout the nineteenth century. In 1854, Herbert Spencer wrote that it was time to dispense once and for all the idea that a tree could be used to represent knowledge (Trompf, 2011). He writes specifically against the notion of the sciences as the 'branches of one trunk', suggesting the notion that 'the sciences had a common origin' is fundamentally flawed.

In short, according to many nineteenth-century Western thinkers, knowledge was not a rooted thing but an uprooted network: a non-hierarchical and non-genealogical interconnected web. For Herbert Spencer, the relationships between the sciences needed to be represented in a more multidimensional way (Van den Heuvel, 2012). What replaced the unity of knowledge was not disconnected chaos, however, but an organisa-tion of knowledge into separate, distinct, and loosely connected disciplines (Yeo, 1991), as evidenced by the various classification systems and institu-tional department structures that cropped up by the late nineteenth and early twentieth centuries. Most classification systems retained some internal hierarchies, but they lacked a common trunk and existed only for organisa-tional convenience rather than to express something deep and true about how concepts related.

In the late nineteenth and early twentieth centuries, ontological discus-sions flourished, perhaps growing in the light once obscured by the dense trees of generations prior. Some hoped to regrow those trees to different purposes, while others sought for new metaphors that eschewed hierarchy, unity, and singular order.

One well-known attempt to eschew hierarchy in classification systems was co-created by the Belgian information activist Paul Otlet near the end of the nineteenth century. Using combinable facets, this Universal Decimal Classification scheme took the multidimensionality of knowledge relation-ships into account far better than the earlier strict tree hierarchies. Otlet sought to represent this multidimensionality visually, intentionally breaking with the arboreal visual metaphors of the past in lieu of more mechanical diagrams, as shown in Figure 7. While he employed a large variety of visual techniques, many of Otlet's illustrations featured non-hierarchical network-like representations of classification with circuitous paths and no discernible trunk or preferred hierarchy (Smiraglia & Van den Heuvel, 2011). For Otlet,

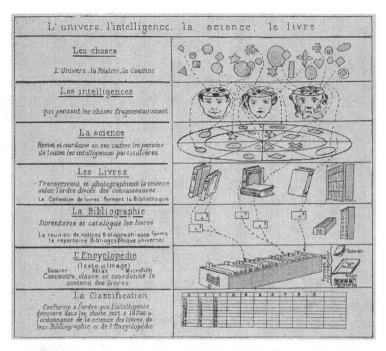

Figure 7 One of Paul Otlet's classification systems, 'L'univers, l'intelligence, la science, le livre', from *Traité de documentation: le livre sur le livre, théorie et pratique* (Editiones Mundaneum, 1934). Digital image. Wikimedia Commons. Public domain.

this classification scheme would ideally lead to 'an immense map of the domains of knowledge' (Otlet, 1918). Otlet's work inspired many others, including S. R. Ranganathan, who in 1933 created a classification scheme which allows knowledge to be classified flexibly and in many dimensions. These new information schemes and metaphors became part of a movement to usher in a future without hierarchies, championed by H. G. Wells and others, coordinated via a vast network of information and communication.

Such utopic and decentralising movements were not without reactions. Faced with a turmoil of disciplines, a growing scientific community sought to reunify the sciences. These scientists were not seeking order in the transcendental sense, but as part of a plan to exert human control over an increasingly chaotic world. This concern was ever-present in the context of a world at war, and it was memorialised in Yeats' 1920 'The Second Coming':

> Turning and turning in the widening gyre
> The falcon cannot hear the falconer;
> Things fall apart; the centre cannot hold;
> Mere anarchy is loosed upon the world[.]

Among their other goals, eugenicists were at the front of a push to hold the scientific centre. Eugenics was, in a sense, an interdisciplinary kind of teaching, bringing together anthropology, genetics, and social policy, among other communities. The logo for the Second International Eugenics Congress (Figure 8), held at the American Museum of Natural History in New York City, depicts a tree of knowledge. It is notable for several reasons. First and foremost, the science of eugenics sits proudly alone in the tree's crown at the top of the page. The branching roots represent the foundations of disciplines: physiology and anatomy combine to form biology, biology merges with psychology to become genetics, and so on. All of the sciences meet at the trunk to form eugenics, labelled 'the self direction of human evolution', which 'organizes knowledge into a harmonious entity'. The diagram appeared again at the Third International Eugenics Congress in 1932, this time captioned with 'Like a tree eugenics draws its materials from many sources and gives them organic *unity* and *purpose*' (emphasis added). The eugenics movement thus actively sought to reinstate concepts of unity, ontology, and hierarchy of knowledge as they were being unravelled. But, of course, eugenics was much more than a theory of knowledge. From the history of the implementation of eugenic policies, which resulted in segregation, sterilisation, and genocide, we know that the unification of knowledge can be an unwitting bearer of ideological content. This offers further evidence of how difficult it is to separate how we order the world from how we live in it.

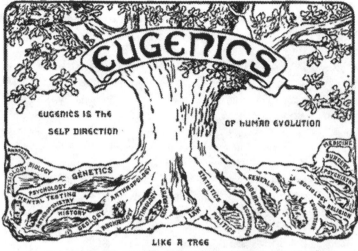

Figure 8 Logo from the Second International Eugenics Conference, 1921, depicting eugenics as a tree which unites a variety of different fields. Harry H. Laughlin, *The Second International Exhibition of Eugenics Held September 22 to October 22, 1921, in Connection with the Second International Congress of Eugenics in the American Museum of Natural History, New York* (Baltimore, MD: William & Wilkins, 1923). Digital image. Wikimedia Commons. Public domain.

It is worth pausing at the turn of the twentieth century to take stock of the state of Western Europe outside of classification theory and of the political context in which particular governments seized upon eugenics. A period of rapid growth in fast, inexpensive transportation and communication networks would soon be punctuated by two world wars. The violent forces of coloni- alism were about to reach a fever peak, and traces of that colonialism were everywhere. The world wars set the backdrop for a renewed fascination with networks of all sorts. Destruction caused by the First World War, alongside a rapidly growing automobile industry and other improving technologies of travel, contributed to prominent discussions of transportation and communication networks. Hungary particularly enjoyed a period of rich international trade, at least until the Great Depression.

It was in this context in 1929 that the Hungarian Frigyes Karinthy wrote 'Láncszemek' ('Chain-Links'), discussed in the previous chapter, which introduced the concept of six degrees of separation. Uncoincidentally, Karinthy's other pursuits included translating H. G. Wells and presiding over the Hungarian Esperanto Society, an organisation in support of a global language for a networked world. The networked ideals of Karinthy, Wells, and Otlet were juxtaposed against a massive push towards hierarchical state-run consolidation exemplified in Nazi sensibilities. When the Nazi librarian Hugo Krüss visited Paul Otlet's Mundaneum in 1940, with its non-hierarchical, sprawling, networked classification system, he considered the whole thing a useless mess. Otlet's ideals and those of his spiritual contemporaries like Karinthy and Wells were an odd mirror to Hitler's. While the juxtaposition of Nazi hierarchies against utopianist networks are far too neat to represent the full story, their interplay is tellingly illustrative. Where Nazis sought to unify people under a powerful hierarchy where individual agency was subordinate to the state, Otlet and others sought unification through a distributed 'World City', connected in peace via networks of information and communication (perhaps sharing a common language, like Esperanto).

Neither goal succeeded. While the latter half of the twentieth century might have steered closer to Otlet's vision than to Hitler's, the twenty-first century might be seen as dealing with the fallout of society's movement towards networks (see Ferguson, 2017). States now continuously fight frontless wars against distributed communities, a synecdoche for the struggle between hierarchies and networks. Recent global political shifts empowering right-wing governments might be seen as a response to this struggle. In this context, the emergence of the network as a framework to challenge traditional hierarchical world views is the product of a long philosophical and cultural crisis stretching from either end of the twentieth century.

As different as they were, the diagrams of eugenicists and those of H. G. Wells shared a common interpretation: that the universe has no innate order and it is left for us to create one. It was in this context that the visual lexicon of the what we now call networks took hold, perhaps because they are the closest ontological metaphor to trees which require neither hierarchy nor root. The way we conceptualise and chart systems of knowledge in the twenty-first century was radically shaped by systems of notation Jacob Moreno and Helen Hall Jennings developed in the 1930s. In their work on social networks (introduced in Chapter 1), Moreno and Jennings developed a psychological technique involving the construction and analysis of *sociograms*, diagrams, like the one shown in in Figure 4, that revealed complex social relations between small communities. At the time, the geometry of these diagrams did not feel obvious. Although they borrowed a visual language from family trees and more recent studies into interpersonal connectivity, it was not necessarily obvious that people should be encircled, that lines ought to connect them, and that their layout on the page should conform neither to physical proximity nor to Cartesian coordinates. Indeed, Moreno and Jennings experimented with many layouts throughout their careers, but sociograms proved the most compelling.

Sociograms enjoyed an intense but brief popularity, showing up in national newspapers in the early 1930s. In these diagrams, Moreno and Jennings suggested that important actors should appear central, and by the late 1940s, the concept of centrality was given mathematical specificity. Alex Bavelas and his colleagues at MIT started connecting centrality with influence and power, focusing especially on the importance of network paths. A central figure, Bavelas argued, sits centrally along the paths to the periphery of a network. Paths are easy to see with sociograms, and Bavelas' early discussions of centrality were unsurprisingly replete with such illustrations. He himself emphasised the role of these visualisations, mentioning that a geometric approach to psychology was only natural in a world where people understand their social world as occupying a physical space around them. Were it not for the precedent of these visual representations, we suspect many early network metrics involving path and centrality would have manifested quite differently.

This visual language of sociograms is now popularised in force-directed layouts. A force-directed layout is a network visualisation that models network elements as though they are physical entities. Edges are modelled as springs, and nodes as junctions connecting various springs together. The computer simulates this system, letting the springs bounce around until each one is as relaxed as possible. At the same time, the nodes repel each other, like magnets of the same polarity, so the nodes do not appear too close together. Just as the tree brought with it implicit notions of hierarchy and unity, this visual language has far-reaching interpretative implications.

Firstly, such visualised networks reject hierarchies. Even when node-and-link diagrams represent hierarchical networks, those hierarchies are difficult to notice. As discussed further in Chapter 4, the lack of any meaningful spatial orientation means even the root node does not occupy a privileged position. Secondly, networks embrace connectedness: in a consilient world, where knowledge collectively acts as a foundation for the whole, or in actor-network theory, where agency can be widely dispersed, this representation fits like a glove. Thirdly, networks separate ontology from essence. Because force-directed networks are stochastic and can therefore look different every time they are constructed, they leave little room to misunderstand a diagram as the one true layout. Knowledge's order is always left uncertain, which feeds into the fourth point: that networks have the capacity to relate situated perspectives. Especially in the past few years, with popular social networks and in-browser interactive force-directed diagrams, it has become possible to view a social network from one's own perspective, which may look very different from the same network represented from someone else's viewpoint. Perspectival visualisations fit remarkably well with feminist and postmodernist understandings of knowledge, and they align poorly with essentialist viewpoints.

The democratising effect of the network view of the world is perhaps most radically realised in actor-network theory (ANT). Despite carrying the label 'theory', ANT is better understood as a range of methodological manoeuvres or processes for guiding research that aims to describe the connections that link humans and non-humans (e.g. objects, technologies, policies, and ideas). It is less concerned with visualising those connections; the ethos is clearly influenced by the non-hierarchical and situated perspective of networks. Actor-network theory is based on the principle that *all* the factors involved in a social situation should be placed on the same level (McLean & Hassard, 2004). Michael Callon's analysis of an investigation into the declining scallop population in St Brieuc Bay outlined a new approach to the study of power, which he described as the sociology of translation (Callon, 1984). Starting from three principles – those of agnosticism (impartiality between actors engaged in controversy), generalised symmetry (the commitment to explain conflicting viewpoints in the same terms), and free association (the abandonment of all a priori distinctions between the natural and the social) – his study examined a scientific and economic controversy about the causes for the decline in the population of scallops in St Brieuc Bay and the attempts by three marine biologists to develop a conservation strategy for that population. One of the notable things about this paper was the way it conceived of the actors in this controversy: in Callon's narrative, the scallops participate with the fishermen and the scientists in a network of associations that undermines any sense of hierarchy of influence.

There is a revolutionary nature to such a conceptual move, as it undermines the celebration of the lone hero, showing that historical change is almost always the result of networks of forces. It is the contention of Bruno Latour's *The Pasteurisation of France*, which asks what one man can accomplish alone. Although every town in France has a street named after Louis Pasteur, he alone was unable to stop people from spitting, persuade them to dig drains, or influence them to undergo vaccination. Rather, Pasteur's success depended upon a network of forces, including the public hygiene movement, the medical profession (both military physicians and private practitioners), and colonial interests. As Annemarie Mol has observed: 'All kind of people, journalists, farmers, technicians, vets, were involved in the discovery/invention of anthrax and the inoculations against it. All kinds of things were active as well, Petri-dishes, blood, transport systems ... Against the implied fantasy of a masterful, separate actor, what is highlighted is the activity of all the associated actors involved. A strategist may be inventive, but nobody acts alone' (Mol, 2010: 256). We can extrapolate a more general argument from this. The process of levelling allows us to challenge other narratives, not only social, but historical, literary, aesthetic, and linguistic, overturning assumptions about causality, hierarchy, the distribution of power, and the direction and quantity of influence.

In these contexts the network perspective is inherently political. There is something decidedly democratic about the initial process that disarms agency and power. It is why early online social networks were praised for their ability to put junior scholars and tenured faculty on equal footing, and why so many of the social movements at the turn of the twenty-first century considered social media a revolutionising force. It may have contributed to the fact that so many early network analysis scholars did not come from traditional places of power.[6] The way network analysis allows us to challenge expected or received wisdom about power dynamics, we contend, also makes it a helpful tool for interrogating the relationship between the humanities and the sociotechnical world in which they operate.

However, the network turn's ability to break existing hierarchical power structures does not imply that it is an acid in which all power melts. Networks reify power along different lines, such as centrality, as evidenced by the enormous power of popular social media presences to gatekeep or to spread certain ideas. The widespread use of network images and methods may be so compellingly effective, in part, because they helped construct the world they purport to measure (see Healy, 2015). Traditional arbiters of power have now learned how to harness network effects to their own advantage. As governments, tech companies, and other centres of power began to take seriously the theories and affordances of networks, they started building the assumptions of those affordances into their systems as a means to re-exert control. As systems start operating on these principles, the world contorts around them to oblige. For example, Google's PageRank algorithm (developed to rank web pages in their search engine results, and the foundation of their success) took web connectivity as a given in a way that fundamentally shaped how web developers thought and acted on hyperlinks. Further, the network processes that were initially hailed as a democratising force have already begun to be strategically employed as an obfuscating layer that hides the reconsolidation of power.

The mantram of the networked modern world is to an extent self-fulfilling: the more we repeat it, the more compellingly appropriate a network lens feels. Without a deeper understanding of the philosophical and rhetorical affordances of the visual forms and conceptual frameworks of networks, we will continue to be unknowingly nudged by their influence.

---

[6] In our research, we discovered that much early sociometry research was undertaken by women and people of colour. So far as we know, this story has never been told, but cannot be in the space available here.

Part II Cultural Networks

By thinking about culture as data we open up opportunities both for new analytical processes and for new areas of discourse and engagement. Arts and humanities scholars need to theorise the construction of data sets and the use of visualisation, which has a challenging and provocative role to play in the development of network approaches to culture.

3 Culture Is Data

The network framework shapes how we interpret the world around us. Nothing is naturally a network; rather, networks are an abstraction into which we squeeze the world. Nevertheless, almost anything can be turned into a network, whether it be the interactions between characters in Shakespeare's plays, the dissemination of memes on Facebook, or the trade network implicated in the ancient Roman brick industry. To understand how such diverse topics can both be conceived of and analysed as networks, it is perhaps easiest to think about one of the most crucial types of network for the creation and dissemination of culture: communication networks. The simple act of communication functions as an entry point for the study of more complex processes such as the dissemination of information or the spread of cultural practices.

We are accustomed to thinking about communication as a network because of the infrastructures that mediate our interactions in the modern world: telephone networks, the World Wide Web, and online social networking platforms. We understand now more than ever that when communication happens through these mediums, it can be traced and measured. Investigations following Edward Snowden's leak in 2013 revealed that the US National Security Agency and its UK counterpart, GCHQ, had 'broadly compromised the guarantees that internet companies have given consumers to reassure them that their communications, online banking and medical records would be indecipherable to criminals or governments' (Ball, Borger, & Greenwald, 2013). Through such data these agencies were able to discover an individual's network of associations and communication patterns. But citizens are not subject only to network analysis in the service of national security: information provided by Christopher Wylie in 2018 confirmed that at least 87 million Facebook users were impacted by illegal data harvesting by Cambridge Analytica, who used this data about users' social networks to profile individual voters during the 2016 Brexit referendum in the UK and the presidential election in the USA in order to target them with personalised political advertisements (Laterza, 2018).

However, a digital trail is not necessary to reconstruct communication networks, and the data sets need not be big. Sociologists were reconstructing networks long before the data deluge. A classic example is Wayne Zachery's observations of a single karate club over three years, from 1970 to 1972, recording interactions between the thirty-four members that took place outside the club (Zachary, 1977). In this context, the members of the club constitute the nodes and the edges are the interactions that occurred between them outside the club: seventy-eight edges were recorded. Zachary used these observations to model the conflict (using the Ford–Fulkerson algorithm) that led ultimately to the club splitting. The emphasis on in-person interaction to model social structure has been appropriated more recently in literary studies, for example in the now much-cited (and much-critiqued) *Literary Lab* pamphlet 'Network Theory, Plot Analysis', in which Franco Moretti attempts to reconstruct the plot of *Hamlet* as a network graph wherein two characters share an edge when they exchange words. He uses the resulting network diagram to argue for the plot centrality of Horatio (Moretti, 2011).

Letters offer perhaps the most intuitive way of reconstructing analogue communication networks. Scholars in the field of epistolary studies have increasingly turned to network analysis and visualisation methods, and all of the authors of this book have worked on this material over the past decade. These efforts include projects on the underground communications between English Protestants during the Catholic reign of Mary and how they kept a community united whilst it was under systematic religious persecution (Ahnert & Ahnert, 2015); the way correspondence networks and scholarly institutions co-evolved into an incredibly efficient machinery for scientific coordination and discovery in early modern Europe (Weingart, under review); the infrastructure of the intelligence networks that underpinned Tudor domestic and foreign policy (Ahnert & Ahnert, 2019); and the role of mapping and visualisation technologies in understanding the intellectual communities of the Republic of Letters (Edelstein et al., 2017, Coleman, 2020). The aims of these various projects are manifold, but they are guided by the desire to find ways to make very large data sets more tractable and to reveal global patterns about how people communicated. The infrastructure of communication networks can be viewed in multiple dimensions, the two most obvious being geographical and social. On the social level, these projects are concerned with people who might bridge communities and geographies in ways that make the world smaller – diplomats, travelling scholars, merchants, or adventurers – which can be discovered using certain combinations of computational measures described in Chapter 5. On the geographic level, scholars can use this data to understand the physical infrastructure that allowed these communications to happen, the veins and arteries of roads along which these communications travelled; what it can tell us about the efficacy of courier systems, early postal systems, and sea routes; or which people were in the same location at the same time.

More abstractly, such work can help us to think about how we can model the spread of information, news, ideas, and concepts across space and time. Yann Ryan's work on the development of the newspaper industry in the early modern period has shown how we can model the movement of individual news items across Europe, as in the case of a story from the *Moderate Intelligencer*, a London newsbook, datelined Hamburg, 21 July 1649, which narrates the war between the Polish and the Cossacks: 'As of old in the War of Alexander and the Romans, so lately in Ireland, and in this, it appears, that it's not the multitude that overcomes, but the wisdome and valour of men, of a very numerous Army, a few usually turns the Scale.' 'How could a writer of news', Ryan asks, 'based in Hamburg, writing about war in Poland, know about the wars in Ireland?' (Ryan, 2018). Building on research into the pan-European nature of the flow of news, Ryan's work seeks to show Britain and Ireland's place within that complex and organic system, how that system can be both local and international, and how it can work with efficiency despite the lack of central planning.

Although parameters of space and time have taken on new dimensions in the era of digital communications, the question of how we model the dissemination of information remains constant. Facebook's research wing has examined the spread of memes on the social networking platform. In a 2016 article, Lada Adamic's team examined the dissemination and evolution of thousands of memes, collectively replicated hundreds of millions of times on Facebook, showing how the information undergoes an evolutionary process that exhibits several regularities, including a power-law (i.e. highly skewed) distribution of memes in variant frequencies. This research also uncovers how subpopulations on the social network 'can preferentially transmit a specific variant of a meme if the variant matches their beliefs or culture' (Adamic et al., 2016). This sense of preferential transmission explains in part why micro-targeting proved such a powerful weapon in the 2016 presidential election and Brexit referendum, but also why research by Soroush Vosoughi, Deb Roy, and Sinan Aral has discovered that fake news disseminates faster and further than the truth. Their data set of rumour cascades on Twitter from 2006 to 2017 (around 126,000 rumours spread by approximately 3 million people) showed that the top 1 per cent of false news cascades diffused to between 1,000 and 100,000 people, whereas the truth rarely reached more than 1,000 people (Vosoughi, Roy, & Aral, 2018).

It is not just information that is disseminated; people move too. In such a context people go from being nodes to being the connecting edges between places, as in the article 'A Network Framework of Cultural History' (and the accompanying video), which provides an overview of the movements of humanity over the past 2,600 years (Schich et al., 2014). The art historian Maximilian Schich and his collaborators on this project used Freebase to find 120,000 individuals who were deemed notable enough in their lifetimes that the dates and locations of their births and deaths were recorded, 'ranging from Solon, the Greek lawmaker and poet, who was born in 637 BCE in Athens, and died in 557 BCE in Cyprus, to Jett Travolta – son of the actor John Travolta – who was born in 1992 in Los Angeles, California, and died in 2009 in the Bahamas' (Abbot, 2014).[7] The team used that data to create a video that starts in 600 BCE and ends in 2012. Each person's birthplace appears on a map of the world as a blue dot and their place of death as a red dot. As a city becomes more important, more notable people die there, identifying these locations as cultural hubs. For example, the data suggests that Paris overtook Rome as a cultural hub in 1789. Schich has argued that the benefit of such a perspective is that 'historians tend to focus in highly specialised areas … but our data allow them to see unexpected correlations between obscure events never considered historically important, and shifts in migration' (Abbot, 2014).

---

[7] Schich and colleagues address potential biases in their data in the supplementary material of their publication, including 'biographical, temporal, and spatial coverage; curated versus crowd-sourced data; increasing numbers of individuals who are still alive; place aggregation; location name changes and spelling variants; and effects of data set language'.

Such a framework is generalisable, offering different approaches for large-scale questions. If we conceptualise the individual people within this aggregate model of migration as carriers, we can imagine how researchers could use the framework Schich proffered to chart how patterns of travel and migration disseminate particular materials, technologies, practices, or concepts. The framework also shares important parallels with the work of the GLEAM project at Northeastern University, which has developed an epidemic forecaster that predicts how given diseases might spread by combining data on population, transport networks, the characteristics of disease, and possible responses (like travel restrictions and vaccination efforts). Using this information, the forecaster generates a simulation of disease propagation across the globe. The importance of this project lies in its ability to make informed suggestions about when and where to disseminate vaccines to minimise the impact of potentially devastating epidemics. During the COVID-19 pandemic in 2020 GLEAM provided early insights into the most effective mitigation strategies to slow the global spread of the disease.

The predictive power of network-based models is a new horizon for cultural studies. In general we tend to study artefacts or practices already in existence. Of course we may soon find ways and uses for making predictions about the cultural arena of tomorrow. But prediction is equally important for thinking about existing culture where our data are scarce or missing, reframed as interpolation or computationally assisted historiographic guesswork. An example of this is Shawn Graham and Scott Weingart's research on the problem of 'equifinality' faced on archaeological sites: when a network is uncovered but the final shape of that network could have been reached by many potential means (Graham & Weingart, 2015). In the example studied, the nodes in the network were a series of bricks bearing the stamps of certain producers (carrying information concerning the estate on which the brick was made, the brick maker, the landowner, and the year) at separate sites, which pointed towards a trade network. Using agent-based modelling as a kind of counterfactual laboratory, the authors predicted the various possible processes that might have formed the networks apparent in the archaeological evidence. By comparing the networks that would have been predicted by Peter Fibiger Bang's model of the

Roman economy, which he calls the 'imperial Bazaar', against those observed in the archaeological materials, Graham and Weingart showed how scholars can employ counterfactual simulations to probe the limits of historical theories. In this case, the methods of prediction are not used to learn something new, but as a formalised thought experiment to better understand the implications of a theorised historical causal explanation. If the simulated results do not match the historical evidence, it is an indication that one's historical explanation needs further articulation.

The foregoing examples, despite the often complex nature or size of the data under consideration, might nevertheless be considered simple in that they constitute unipartite (or unimodal) networks: that is, networks with nodes of just one type. As we have argued elsewhere, however, the kind of networks humanists are interested in are often more complicated: 'We don't just have people connected to people or websites to websites, we've got people connected to institutions to authored works to ideas to whatever else, and we want to know how they all fit together' (Weingart, 2013). This is where we can employ what are known as multipartite (or multimodal) networks.

The flavour network is a bipartite example. Sebastian Ahnert's research with collaborators at the Barabási Lab was inspired by the food-pairing hypothesis proffered by the chef Heston Blumenthal and the food scientist François Benzi: that ingredients will taste good together in a dish if they share chemical flavour compounds. Until their 2011 article, this hypothesis relied on anecdotal rather than large-scale quantitative evidence (Ahn et al., 2011). Thanks to the efforts of food scientists around the world, we now have extensive information available about the many chemical compounds responsible for giving different foods their distinctive smells and tastes. The two node types generated from that data for the bipartite network are the ingredients (such as garlic, chocolate, coffee, basil) and the individual chemical compounds. In order to show the relationships between a particular set of nodes, bipartite networks are usually transformed by a 'one-mode projection'. This means that the resulting network contains nodes of only one of either of the two sets. In this case, a one-mode projection of the ingredients was generated and edges were created between any foods that shared one or more compounds; the edges between those ingredients were weighted by the number of compounds they shared. The resulting network was then used to test the food-pairing hypothesis by cross-referring it with a data set of 56,498 recipes. This analysis revealed that Western cuisines show a tendency to use ingredient pairs that share many flavour compounds, supporting Blumenthal and Benzi's hypothesis, but East Asian cuisines tend to avoid compound-sharing ingredients. This work shows how systems and hypotheses that do not seem at first sight to be about networks can be approached productively through that framework.

Where might this kind of approach be useful in the humanities? It is particularly pertinent where one has sources or data containing two different types of entities, and especially when one is a subset of (or somehow contained within) the other. For example, if we think of miscellanies – a collection of literary compositions or pieces by several authors assembled in a volume or book – we could create a bipartite network linking texts (node type one) with the miscellanies that contain them (node type two). So, in our toy network diagram (Figure 9), if text A appears in miscellanies X, Y, and Z, and text B appears in miscellanies Y and Z, then the bipartite network has connections A-X, A-Y, A-Z, B-Y, and B-Z. By then undertaking a one-mode projection of texts connected by miscellanies, we can see which texts appear together in such miscellanies (middle), or conversely, by projecting this as a network of miscellanies connected by shared texts, we can see how closely particular miscellanies are related to one another (bottom). Scaling up this idea, we can begin to see how an analysis of all catalogued Renaissance poetry miscellanies might enable us to understand the early modern poetic universe in different ways. It could tell us which poems most commonly appeared together, it might help us see which manuscripts were most similar in their contents, and it may uncover patterns of scribal circulation.

An example of this kind of bipartite thinking can be found in Richard Jean So and Hoyt Long's analysis of the publication networks of early twentieth-century poets. In their analysis, the two node types are poets and journals, and the fact of publication in the same journal is the edge linking one type of node to another. Their aim was the interrogation of the social dimensions of early twentieth-century poetry production in the United States, Japan, and China. 'The little magazines and independent coterie

bipartite network of texts and miscellanies:

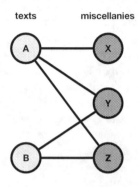

texts   miscellanies

---

projected network of texts:

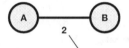

edge weight indicating
two shared miscellanies, Y and Z

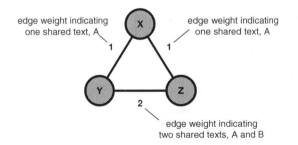

projected network of miscellanies:

edge weight indicating
one shared text, A

edge weight indicating
one shared text, A

edge weight indicating
two shared texts, A and B

Figure 9 A simple example of a bipartite network made up of nodes and miscellanies (top) projected as a network of texts (middle), and projected as a network of miscellanies (bottom). Diagram by the authors.

journals of the time were essential mechanisms for organizing creativity, collaboration, and the transnational diffusion of poetic styles' (So & Long, 2013: 157). Their work identifies key brokers in literary circles that include key writers (such as Amy Lowell and Countee Cullen in the network of American poets, 1924–5), and journals (such as *Shishin* in the network of Japanese journals, 1927–9).

For humanities scholars unfamiliar with the network framework, the breadth and inclusivity of the foregoing examples may be surprising. Without the metaphorical and analytic power of networks, it is difficult to understand how the interactions of characters in *Hamlet* are in any way comparable to the dissemination of memes on Facebook, or the chemical compounds shared between food ingredients. What makes them comparable is an intellectual and methodological shift by which we abstract our objects of study into data points that can be entered into a database or spreadsheet. This does not imply some shared property intrinsic to each of the subjects under study, rather it implies the widespread utility of networks as a lens through which to view many aspects of our shared world.

The idea of talking about cultural artefacts as data, metadata, or data sets is in itself a potentially controversial move as it seems reductive, ignoring complexity, ambiguity, and qualitative assessment. Moreover, as Johanna Drucker has argued, the etymology of the word 'data' is itself problematic in the context of the arts and humanities: it comes from the Latin *datum*, which means 'that which is given'. The word 'data' therefore carries with it the meaning of an observer-independent fact which cannot be challenged in itself. Drucker prefers instead to think in terms of 'capta': 'that which has been captured or gathered', a coinage designed to draw attention to the fact that the very act of capturing data is oriented by certain goals, done with specific instruments, and driven by a specific attention to a small part of what could have been captured given different goals and instruments (Drucker, 2011). In other words, it requires decisions and interpretations that introduce subjectivity into the process. Throwing out the word 'data' completely, however, seems unwise given its ubiquity and acceptance across disciplines, especially if one of our aims is to create discourses and practices that break down traditional disciplinary divides. It is perhaps best, therefore, to make sure that scholars from the arts and humanities are not held captive to assumptions about what data is, and rather play an active role in applying a self-reflexive and theoretical lens to the act of data creation and capture and its subsequent processing, not just in the humanities and arts, but across the disciplines. Dan Rosenberg's work on the history of data zeros in on the distinctions between data, fact, and evidence. He writes, 'facts are ontological, evidence is epistemological, data is rhetorical,' which means that 'the existence of a datum has been independent of any consideration of corresponding ontological truth' (Rosenberg, 2013: 18). Rosenberg's formulation helps us to see that data are what we determine them to be, but we do need to take responsibility to define them clearly.

Two key issues for network data are those of absence and 'bias' (broadly defined). The concern we hear repeated most often by our colleagues in the arts and humanities is that the incompleteness or complexity of their source material make it unsuitable for network analysis. The concern arises, in part, from a misconception about what 'scientific' data looks like. It is important to remember, however, that almost any network data set, even in the sciences, is incomplete in some sense. In whatever way we define the connection between entities and the entities themselves, we are limited by the scope of available data and by the assumptions made when defining the nature of the connections. While this of course will affect the results of any quantitative analysis, this incompleteness is less of a problem than it may seem at first, for three main reasons.

The first reason is that, particularly in the context of the humanities, the bias in the source data is often itself of interest to the scholar. When we look at cultural phenomena and artefacts, we look at them with particular well-theorised frames. However, for much data we do not have a well-thought-out, critical apparatus to describe the 'how', 'who', and 'what' of the data, so it is not clear whether we are analysing a particular phenomenon, some artefact of the collection and accumulation process, or our own world views. For example, in the case of archives of historic documents, network analysis can help the researcher to better understand the history of that archive by drawing attention to deliberate inclusions or omissions of material, perhaps motivated by a political or religious collection agenda, the confiscation of documents, or even the deliberate destruction or censorship of materials.

Such events in the history of an archive are detectable precisely because of the effects they have of distorting the results of the quantitative analysis. We might be able to extrapolate similar kinds of lessons for survival or loss of archaeological evidence. And more generally, it could help in the development of a consistent scholarly apparatus for understanding the peculiarities of digital archives and databases. Via source criticism, we still only know in the broadest strokes the implications of their formation and shape for the research we undertake. Articulating humanities network data in these terms, as a perspective rather than a 'bias' – which implies some underlying ground truth – will be a grand challenge for the next generation of researchers in this area.

The second reason is that, even in an incomplete network, the relative importance of nodes and edges according to a given network measurement can still yield meaningful results. Every network data set analysed in network science, be it a mobile phone network, a network between genes, or an online social network, is incomplete or limited by selection. But the limited scope in which the data is collected does not prohibit us from examining the relative importance of nodes or edges in the context of that scope, as long as we are aware of the factors that may shape our results.

The third and most important reason why the incompleteness of networks does not pose an insurmountable problem is that the results of the quantitative analysis do not serve as a final result, but as a starting point for further, more detailed inquiry in the vein of traditional scholarship in the arts and humanities. In Chapter 6, we provide a guide through what this might mean practically for the research process.

The message that networks do not need to be complete should not be used to discount the problem of inconsistent sampling or poor data gathering. But network analysis can be part of the answer if it is employed as a tool for characterising the contours of a given archive or corpus, thereby helping to show how the data with which we work so often reinscribes structural bias. This raises an important issue when understanding and constructing cultural objects as data. The big-data approach to culture offers many opportunities, as discussed earlier, but with it comes a duty of care that is at once technical and ethical (Weingart, 2014a). These two aspects are intimately intertwined.

The technical duty of care is often called 'data cleaning', a term used to describe the process of detecting and correcting (or removing) corrupt or inaccurate elements in a given data set. Issues within a single data set or database might be created by misspellings during data entry, missing information, or other invalid data. The term, however, is not without problems, as has been discussed in the provocatively titled piece 'Against Cleaning' (Rawson & Muñoz, 2019). Rawson and Muñoz's point is that the metaphor of cleaning is problematic because it elides the burden of labour and intellectual contribution that it actually represents. They contend that: 'Data cleaning is a consequential step in the research process that we often make opaque by the way we talk about it. The phrase "data cleaning" is a stand-in for longer and more precise descriptions of what people are doing in the initial phases of data-intensive research.' The lack of discussion around such practices, they argue, has increased mistrust of quantitative approaches in the arts and humanities. The only way to deal with this is to begin talking about the labour of cleaning and to communicate its significance as an intellectual contribution.

One example is the preparation Ruth and Sebastian Ahnert undertook for the Tudor Networks of Power project. Their primary data set was a digitised archive, State Papers Online (SPO), which combines scans of the British State Papers archive with the Calendar descriptions of their contents. It provides metadata for each document that, in the case of the letters on which they were working (numbering circa 132,000 items for the Tudor period), contains valuable relational information including: name of sender, name of recipient, date of composition, place of writing, unique document identifiers, and a content description. The author, recipient, and place fields in particular needed cleaning. In the case of the author and recipient fields, the names needed disambiguation and de-duplication, for a number of reasons: variant spellings of early modern names, letters addressed to a titular office rather than a named individual (e.g. the Archbishop of Canterbury), changing office holders, changing titles over a person's lifetime as they accrued honours and offices, and women's names changing due to marriage. The complexity of the sender and recipient metadata fields meant that although 37,101 unique name entities were initially extracted, there were in fact only 20,656 unique correspondents. Place names had to be dealt with in a similar way and geo-coordinates added. This effort led to the development of two custom data cleaning tools. In addition, the curation of those data fields involved eighteen months of work (Hyvönen et al., 2019; Ahnert & Ahnert, forthcoming: chapter 1). This is a considerable workload that needed to be undertaken before network analysis could even be contemplated and the results of quantitative analysis could be trusted. This work should not just be considered a prerequisite for network analysis or other quantitative approaches, however, but a scholarly object in its own right: a data set other researchers can put to many uses. A cultural shift in the humanities is still required before such work is given the scholarly credit it deserves.

A vital by-product of this labour is that during the process researchers become intimately acquainted with the shape of their data, its strengths, weaknesses, and biases. This is where the ethical duty of care comes in. Lauren F. Klein's MLA paper on 'Distant Reading after Moretti' argued that we need to look at our data to understand why 'distant reading does not deal well with gender, or with sexuality, or with race.' She suggests that we need data sets that:

> perform the work of recovery or resistance. An example: the corpus created by the Colored Conventions Project, which seeks to recover and aggregate evidence that documents the Colored Conventions of the nineteenth-century United States; these were organizing meetings in which Black Americans, both fugitive and free, came together to strategize about how to achieve social and legal justice. By making this corpus available for others to download, the CCP opens up the project of distant reading to texts beyond quote 'representative' samples, which tend to reproduce the same inequities of representation that affect our cultural record as a whole. (Klein, 2018)

Attending to the biases created in the creation of the archives with which we work allows us to address them. Networks can be part of that process, helping us to describe the data we have, and therefore allowing us to see where gaps and skews are present and to think critically about the ways in which they may be addressed.

By thinking about the culture around us as data we therefore not only open up opportunities for new analytical processes, we also identify an important way in which arts and humanities scholars can contribute critically to the ways we theorise the construction of data sets. The ways that this community is accustomed to thinking about these objects of study offers a different perspective on the status of data, its capture, preparation, shape, strengths and weakness, as well as the duty of care required to ensure it is fit for purpose. As the next chapter argues, one of the ways we can interrogate our data is through the lens of visualisation.

4 *Visual Networks*

Visual networks are compelling, but are they effective? The conventional network graph of node and edge (points connected by lines) makes it possible to convey a tremendous amount of information all at once, in one view. Networks express an internal logic of relationships between entities that is inherently intuitive. But they also lack an explicit external spatial referent, whether the latitude and longitude of cartography, the scale and sequence of a timeline, or the categories and measures that mark the x-y axis of a statistical graph. They can represent relationships at human visible scale, or scale to dizzying, visually indecipherable complexity. The unbounded rhizomatic structure of the network has a malleable, infinitely re-orderable form that communicates in a way that is distinct from almost all other diagrams of data. This chapter addresses how that malleability can be harnessed for research and communication.

The sketch presented in Figure 10 is one of many drafts leading up to Mark Lombardi's work, 'BCCI-ICIC & FAB, 1971–91 (4th Version)', with which we opened this book. It is a rough, incomplete, marked-up draft with nodes outlined in blue, connections crossed out, and empty spaces awaiting more information. A comparison between this draft and the final version gives us some insight into the evolution of Lombardi's thinking. Externalising information and organising ideas spatially is not just a mode of presentation, it is an integral part of Lombardi's research into these complex financial systems. The story he finally shares has been refined through the process of sketching, editing, and redrawing. But it is not merely a cleaned-up version of the draft. It demonstrates Lombardi's command of visual rhetoric to lay out his argument for public consumption; to convince and persuade with his choice of colour, the quality of the line, the careful annotation, the apparent precision, the internal structure, and the overall shape. The fragments of evidence Lombardi originally collected on three-by-five notecards and arranged in notes and sketches do not speak for themselves; they are selected, edited, and enriched, using visualisation at stages throughout the process as a cognitive aide, a modelling activity, an argument, and a work of art in turn (see Tversky & Suwa, 2009 and Tversky, 2014). It is an iterative act of knowledge production that if executed in prose rather than in drawing would

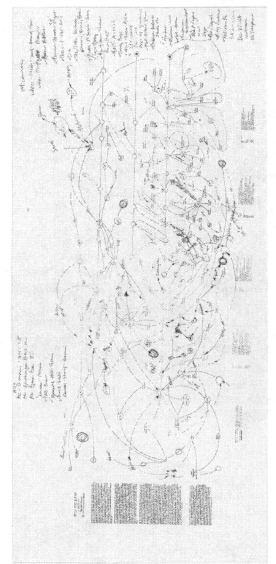

Figure 10 Lombardi, Mark (1951–2000): Untitled from the series BCCI, ICIC & FAB, 1996. Pen and ink and electrophotographic print on paper. New York, Whitney Museum of American Art. © 2019. Digital image. Whitney Museum of American Art / Licensed by Scala. figure 1

be very familiar to humanities scholars. This familiarity is an important point of reference when comparing hand-drawn visual networks like Lombardi's to those drawn with computer graphics software. Ben Fry, for example, points to Lombardi's work for lessons in a humanist view of data that uses visualisation as a story-telling medium requiring significant editing (Fry, 2016). Our contention is that handled in the right way, network visualisation can be both an important means of knowledge production and a powerful rhetorical tool.

The role of the visual in the production of knowledge is the thesis of Johanna Drucker's *Graphesis*. She opens the book with a comparison of two network visualisations: Athanasius Kircher's *Ars magna sciendi* (1669) and Barrett Lyon's 'Web Traffic Visualisation'. Both are networks depicted as nodes and edges (see Figure 11). Kircher returns us to the diagrammatic approaches to knowledge discussed in Chapter 2. It is a development of Ramon Llull's system published in his *Ars generalis ultima* or *Ars magna*: a method of combining religious and philosophical attributes selected from a number of lists, designed to engage Muslims in debate and win them to the Christian faith. Kircher's diagram forms a complete bipartite graph, where every node of the first set is connected to every node of the second. The Lyon visualisation, part of his Opte Project, is a computer-generated network graph intended to map the Internet. Nodes represent individual servers and hosts, and edges represent the fibre, copper, or other connections between them. Drucker's purpose in juxtaposing these two graphs is to draw our attention to their relationship to information. Kircher's work, she argues, '*produces the knowledge it draws*': the effect of combination is to generate insights. By comparison, Lyon's network visualisation of web traffic 'only displays information'. This distinction is an important one when thinking about how we employ visualisation in our work. Off-the-shelf graphics packages are employed in research as a means both of generating insights and displaying observed phenomena. However, the word 'display' is a potentially misleading term. As Drucker puts it, certain visualisations 'act as if they are just showing us *what is*, but in actuality, they are *arguments made in graphical form*' (Drucker, 2014). We need to recognise the rhetorical power of visualisation if we are to remain alert to the hidden agendas of the graphical forms we encounter.

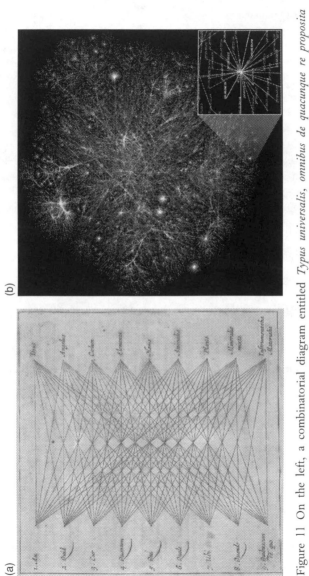

Figure 11 On the left, a combinatorial diagram entitled *Typus universalis, omnibus de quacunque re proposita questionibus formandis, aptus*, in Athanasius Kircher, *Ars magna sciendi* (Janssonius a Waesberg, 1669). Digital image. Max Planck Institute for the History of Science Library. CC BY SA 3.0. On the right, a visualisation from the Opte Project of the various routes through a portion of the Internet in 2005. Digital image. Wikimedia Commons. CC BY 2.5.

We can begin to understand how arguments are made in graphical form by looking at a set of diagrams based on the networks chapter of Jacques Bertin's *The Semiology of Graphics* (Figure 12). Bertin defines a general theory of graphics as separate from both figurative representation and mathematics. While Bertin employs some problematic assumptions about both the certainty of data and the 'monosemic' system of graphical rhetoric, his work is nevertheless a crucial study for our thinking about different insights, and consequently the arguments that can be made through different diagrammatic layouts of network data.

The network, according to Bertin, is represented by three components: the line, the point, and the area. He specifies a number of possible layouts making use of those components including rectilinear, circular, irregular arrangement, and regular arrangement (see Figure 12). Each combination of components and arrangements highlights different aspects of the data and contributes to a different argument about the underlying data. The tabular view provides the basic source–target pairs. The 'irregular arrangement' is the familiar, decentred layout most often associated with visual networks. It does not spatially prioritise any node and yet, with a network this small, we can quickly assess that A, B, C, and E are more connected than the other nodes. The 'regular arrangement' explicitly sets A as the root node in a tree-like hierarchy. The top-to-bottom order of the horizontal planes of alignment is clearly intentional and insists on a particular reading of the graph, even if the significance is not made explicit. And whereas the 'regular arrangement' gives prominence to A, the circular layout emphasises the node with the most connections. The lines radiating out from C give it a visually significant role in the network even though all the nodes are aligned on a periphery. The rectilinear layout suggests a sequence to the connections and makes clear, with this particular data set, that E connects more nodes along the chain than any other node (which, as we see in Chapter 5, would mean it has the highest betweenness centrality). The parallel alignment diagram and the matrix reveal directionality and absence more explicitly than the network graphs because they both draw corresponding connections between two fixed planes. Since these two layouts accommodate all possible connections, they draw our attention to where there are

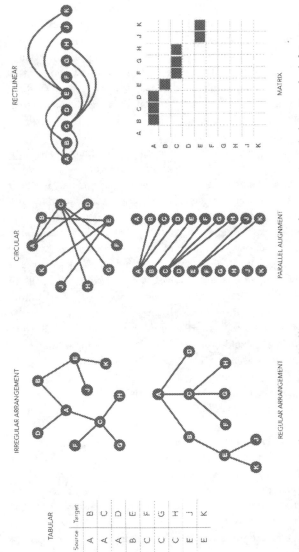

Figure 12 This figure shows a number of different ways to present the same network data. On the left is source–target pairs in a two-column table. The regular and irregular arrangement, circular, and rectilinear are all network layouts in Bertin's system. He distinguishes those node-link network graphs from the diagrams: parallel alignment and matrix. Diagram by the authors.

none. Even with this simple overview, it quickly becomes apparent how much the arrangement of nodes influences our reading of a network.

What is useful about Bertin's work is that it gives us a point of reference for reading the rhetoric encoded in design decisions. For example, if we return to Lombardi, we can see Lombardi's drawings align with Bertin's rules and extend them in unique ways. Lombardi's networks are hand drawn with a fine black line on white paper, sometimes accented with red, with descriptive labels and notes. He distinguishes six different types of connection between nodes: 1) influence or control in one direction, 2) mutual connection, 3) financial connection, 4) sale or transfer of assets, 5) a blocked or incomplete transfer, and 6) the sale or spin-off of a property. Moreover, Lombardi uses the rectilinear arrangement of nodes to add a temporal dimension to the visual network. In some cases, instead of a one-to-one relationship between node and entity, an organisation (usually a financial institution) is represented as a horizontal line with a beginning and an end. These are the primary entities, depicted as chronologies rather than singular nodes. The differences in the quality of the lines (solid, dashed, broken, twisted) are difficult to see at a distance, making the scale of his work an important part of the experience of it (the final work is 129.9 cm x 349.9 cm). Stepping back from the work, it is possible to take it all in as a complete system. The labels and notes are not legible at that distance, though the lines and vertices are clear. Even if the temporality is not explicitly visible, the horizontal lines add another layered dimension to the connectedness. A distant reading complements the close reading. Standing next to the work, the different types of connection and the handwritten labels and notes are easy to see. It encourages the reader to follow paths through the network, shifting their own position in relation to the artwork.

Researchers have made attempts to automate Lombardi's layout, to capture it as a reproducible algorithmic process. Indeed, there is a significant body of work in graph drawing studies called 'Lombardi drawings' (e.g. see Duncan et al., 2010). Such attempts, however, ignore the real value of his drawings and what is at stake in their creation. Lombardi was interested in evidence-based *visual* argument (the 'narrative structure') about specific individuals and organisations engaged in particular types of relationship over time. And his sketching process, leading up to the final presented work, captures the process of formulating that argument. Conversely, software programs for visualisation use predefined graphics libraries where much of the decision-making is pre-baked into the tool. They therefore take out of the user's hands the experience of the roughly drawn sketch as part of a generative and exploratory thought process. Instead, it jumps right into the visually precise presentation that we associate with the argument. It is not only that computer graphics look precise, computer graphics software is encoded with assumptions about graphical meaning rooted in Bertin's theory of graphics as monosemic and unambiguous.

Just because visualisation tools present results to us in ways that can be understood as deterministic does not mean we need to use them that way. But we do need to be aware of the assumptions encoded in the tools we use so that we can bend them to our own needs. What follows is a comparison of two network visualisation packages often used in the humanities: Palladio and Gephi. Palladio uses interaction, filtering, and complementary visualisation modes to facilitate the exploration of multidimensional data sets. Gephi uses dynamic simulation to apply layout algorithms to generate graph network visualisations. The comparison is guided by what we expect to gain from the visualisation of data. Isabel Meirelles uses the words 'descriptive' and 'argumentative' to distinguish between visualisation for the exploration of data and visualisation for the communication of findings. She is careful to note that these are not either/or categories, but two poles of a continuum. Descriptive visualisation, Meirelles writes, is a reflection of direct mappings of the data – the who, what, where, and when – whereas argumentative visualisation tends to the more speculative (Meirelles, 2018). This approach to visualisation foregrounds our relationship to the data to be visualised. Lombardi's BCCI project and some of his collected data are the common point of reference in our comparison to help reveal the advantages and potential pitfalls of using software-generated visual networks in the research process.

Palladio is a toolset rooted in an historical-cultural orientation to network analysis that is more art than science. It is the result of experimentation with custom-made visualisations designed to answer specific historical questions about the shape of political, social, and intellectual communities in the early modern period (Edelstein et al., 2017; Coleman, 2020). The techniques deemed successful in those experiments were distilled and combined into one suite of tools. The result is a basic force-directed bipartite network graph embedded within an interactive and interchangeable set of data views that includes a geospatial view, a tabular view, and filtering on temporal and categorical dimensions. The interactive tools are designed to work together to help reveal many types of connectedness by facilitating multiple different points of view combined with faceting and filtering on different dimensions of the data. It is assumed that no one view is complete, but that a more complete picture is understood as much by seeing what is missing as by seeing the extant data (see Rendgen & Weidemann, 2012: 155; Uboldi et al., 2013).

An exploration of Lombardi's data set with Palladio, for example, might begin with a map of the known locations. The text printed on the side of Lombardi's *Untitled* sketch (Figure 10) indicates that BCCI was the brainchild of a Pakistani banker based in Karachi. The bank was controlled from Abu Dhabi, was incorporated in Luxembourg, was operated from London, Geneva, and the Cayman Islands, and was involved in joint ventures with local banks in Iran, Oman, France, and Switzerland. Since BCCI was, according to Lombardi, the legitimate front for the shadowy ICIC, examining the locations of individuals he believed were involved could reveal potential connections that might spur further research. Adding the time span filter in Palladio would make the data Lombardi has about when the entities formed and dissolved, cross-referenced with the timeline of specific dates when particular individuals met or financial transactions were recorded, available to filter, making it possible to quickly and easily zero in on which activities are taking place where and at what time. And since Lombardi seems to have more information about the relationships between people and organisations than about locations, he can look at the same filtered subset of data in a graph view to reveal connections between individuals and organisations at those moments in time.

This example demonstrates how Palladio can be used for sketching, in the sense of exploring, or thinking through data as a cognitive aid. It aids cognition by combining visualisations with the counting of values and categories that can easily be grouped and regrouped, arranged and rearranged. The faceting and filtering combines with the visual description to enable a subtle interrogation of heterogeneous, multidimensional data sets by concept and duration rather than purely numeric values. It was designed to be used with historical and archival data, with the assumption of incompleteness and uncertainty in the sources. Successful use of Palladio therefore requires the researcher to make inferences based on the visualised data, but it leaves space for the expert to fill in the gaps in the many cases where their knowledge of the subject extends beyond the data collected. It minimises automatic animation in favour of explicitly selected actions, to encourage reflection as views are reoriented and data is manipulated. The application is there not to run an analytical model but to facilitate modelling, to create space for assessment and imagination.

Gephi, by comparison, was developed in the context of the interdisciplinary *e-Diasporas* project to analyse online migrant communities (Diminescu, 2012). The underlying data, referred to as an *e-diaspora corpus*, is a list of diasporic websites selected by the project authors. The tool reflects the project's interest in the power of network science and the desire to visually expose network topology. Its creators describe it as the Photoshop of network graphs and it uses computer simulations to show layout algorithms acting on network data (Bastian, Heymann, & Jacomy, 2009). The force-directed layouts are a class of algorithms used frequently in Gephi and the visual form with which readers will be most familiar because of their increasing ubiquity through high-volume use of Gephi and similar tools. In a force-directed layout, each element of the network is modelled as though guided by unseen forces, much as in the physical world: gravity, electromagnetic repulsion, material elasticity. Nodes may be thought of as electrons on a two-dimensional plane, forcing each other apart as they approach one another, and the edges may be conceived of as springs physically anchored between two nodes, drawing them together even as they repulsively push away. The plane has no meaning; there are no axes defining categories against which to measure node position. But as we are already aware, we do come to these resulting images with a set of assumptions about meaning. Gephi also allows users to apply a whole range of quantitative measures (discussed further in Chapter 5) and then colour or resize visual elements according to those attributes.

An analysis of Lombardi's data set with Gephi would make it possible to automatically generate a calculated layout based on the connectedness of nodes in his network. Layout models embedded in a software application are extremely powerful. It makes it easy to quickly apply a given model to lots and lots of data. However, by making it so easy to apply multiple different layouts to the same data set, small data problems can be overlooked and amplified. In the scientific context, where network analysis is based on equations and resulting measures, computer-generated graphics like those produced with Gephi have come under scrutiny for unnecessarily introducing ambiguity into a reading of network topology. The argument is that spatial arrangements, colours, shapes, and labels complicate measurements that are more clearly presented numerically. But the source of confusion in network graphics resulting from powerful visualisation tools like Gephi may have more to do with the fact that visualisation is too often learned rather than taught. Too often users allow the software to determine the layout or become enamoured of the visualisation and animation, losing sight of the intent to accomplish something on the spectrum of description to argument.

Tommaso Venturini, Mathieu Jacomy, and Pablo Jensen have begun to address this challenge by explicitly defining the strengths and weaknesses of what they have called visual network analysis (VNA) and providing guidelines for how to make effective use of algorithmic layouts to expose the topological structure of large networks (Venturini, Jacomy, & Jensen, 2019). The diagrammatic network layouts Bertin offered – which provide visual clarity through either symmetry or minimising overlapping connections – break down when networks reach the size of several hundred or thousands of nodes. The argument underlying VNA is that understanding the conceptual and mathematical underpinnings of the layout algorithms and choosing appropriate settings can result in effective, legible graph spatialisation. Even though the specific position of each node on the plane is not relevant, the density (or lack of density) of nodes is. And though the structure of the visualised graph does not strictly correlate with the underlying mathematical calculations of the network, the structure that emerges through polarisation of nodes, even in a very large network, functions effectively as exploratory data analysis (Tukey, 1977). Selectively highlighting variables in the data reveal patterns. Nodes can be sized according to degree measures (see Chapter 5);

brightness can be applied to continuous numerical variables and hue for categorical variables. And just as with the experience of Lombardi's drawing, here closeness and distance are both revealing: zooming in and out in a Gephi visualisation makes global and local patterns visible. Even if the end goal is not a statistical reading of the network, the statistical readings available through Gephi provide intellectual prompts to examine your data in new ways.

Lombardi's work, Palladio, and Gephi represent three different kinds of visual engagement with data that require and deliver different levels of artistry, control, and quantitative engagement, but all of them encourage an important process of exploration. Network visualisations are often critiqued as either overly reductive (in terms of content and context) or absurdly illegible (in terms of visual complexity), yet they bring an immediacy to our perception of information. Graphics as a system for the creation and presentation of knowledge requires our attention. Graphics can, and often are, used throughout a research process from sketch drawings that help us build intuitions about connectivity, to descriptive data visualisation, to visual arguments in a final publication. Though data analysis is widely considered synonymous with particular forms of visualisation these days, charts and graphs were not widely accepted until they were formalised in the mid-twentieth century when computing and, specifically, computational information processing was on the rise. Statisticians Jacques Bertin and John Tukey, whose careers spanned the latter half of the twentieth century, were both pioneering figures who solidified the role of visualisation in providing insights that would otherwise be missed in mathematical data analysis. Bertin anticipated that the automation computers provide in calculation, combined with the ability to transform and reorder via computer display, would enable visualisation of much larger data sets. He seemed confident that computer graphics would be the apotheosis of his goal to produce 'the simplest and thus most communicable image'. However, one could argue that the ideal Bertin imagined has gotten away from us.

Cultural phenomena that Bertin could not have anticipated have radically changed our relationship to data graphics. Our day-to-day familiarity with mapping services is a case in point. We not only accept but rely upon their cartographic conventions to reduce the complexity of the landscape in order to serve a particular purpose: wayfinding. We navigate from point to point, implicitly accepting the abstraction of the map because we have our embodied experience of walking, riding, and driving streets to fill in the gaps. We know that travel between two nodes is rich and layered; it is never a straight line. We have learned to reframe space in scale from a global view to the city streets with longitude and latitude and familiar geography as a guide. We trust these constantly shifting maps perhaps because we are so aware of their limitations or because we rely on their convenience. As a result, we allow ourselves to be led by them, unaware of or tacitly accepting their encoded intention. The intervention of software as an unseen hand in the construction of visualisations presents new challenges to our reading of them. When the direct connection between the author and the output is not evident in the form, we can be seduced into experiencing visualisation as objective. This is even more likely when the map layer is removed and what is left is a visualised network graph without a physical referent.

Spatialisation of nodes and links, vectors and vertices, without reference to scale or familiar geospatial markers is unsettling and confrontational. And yet, eschewing the Cartesian hand-holds of the map reveals patterns and movement that would otherwise be obscured or overshadowed by the expectations we bring to the geospatial framing of data. It focuses our attention differently – from topography to the line and its inherent relation-ships. The points, lines, and areas by themselves can be disorienting and challenge our assumptions about what is significant in the data. At the same time, our relationship to data has changed radically in this century. Not only is there much more of it, it is much more personal. As a result, we are better able to see the human-scale biases and assumptions behind the abstract and inherently fragmented visualisation of networks. Just as networks are always metaphorical, visual networks are as much about schema as they are a set of relationships and measurements. These opportunities and challenges of the network have been seized upon by artists, scholars, and, more recently, the developers of visualisation tools and libraries. The need to concretise the abstract has given way to the desire to communicate expressively now that we have extremely powerful tools with which to fulfil that desire. The challenge is to redefine the role of graphics in network analysis for the future of network science, design, and humanistic inquiry. Dan Rosenberg, for example, posits a different analytic goal of visualisation: 'to complicate rather than simplify, to open multiple avenues of inquiry, and, most importantly, to challenge the stability of underlying data, in fact or in principle' (Rosenberg, 2016).

The fact that dense and complex networks resemble neural connections in the brain, rhizomatic weed roots pulled from the ground, twenty-four hours of airline flight, or the exchange of information over the Internet, communicates something about the very real complexity we experience in our everyday lives at many different scales, which we need to interrogate. We propose that visualisation is not better than narrative argument or mathematical equations for communicating ideas, but that it provides an additional means of producing, exploring, and analysing information that has proven value in both the liberal arts and the sciences. When working with data, visualisation can help reveal gaps that narrative-based research practices do not expose, or uncover qualities in data sets that can easily be overlooked when we focus only on numbers and calculations. Moreover, it is rhetorically powerful. Visualisations of networks are unsettling because the graphical language used to produce them is not, in fact, precise. For these reasons, we argue that visualisation has a challenging and provocative role to play in the development of network approaches to culture, a role that needs to be fully integrated into an iterative and self-reflexive research process. In Part III, we outline the manoeuvres that make up that process.

Part III Manoeuvres

Network analysis provides a set of manoeuvres: intellectual manoeuvres that refigure cultural objects in our minds as abstract systems of nodes and edges; mechanical manoeuvres that structure data and that navigate input versus output; and manoeuvres between a landscape of abstraction and research questions that are steeped in contextual information. These manoeuvres dismantle the binaries between distant and close reading, quantitative and qualitative analysis, the nomothetic and idiographic, and, in so doing, create new norms of practice and inquiry.

5 Quantifying Culture

If network visualisations have a rhetoric, then so do numbers. The perceived shift towards the quantification of humanistic study in recent years has been the subject of ongoing debate. While the quantification of literary culture has a history that stretches back into the 1930s and 1940s – if we accept the standard origin story of humanities computing that cites Josephine Miles and Roberto Busa's collaboration with IBM (Buurma & Heffernan, 2018; Terras & Nyhan, 2016) – the increasing availability of data at scale and our growing reliance on computational discovery since the rise of information technology in the late twentieth century has made the case for quantification more compelling.

Nevertheless, the backlash has been fierce. At the heart of debates around quantification are a set of assumptions about its objectivity, measurability, and reproducibility that need to be (productively) challenged and problematised. Naïve arguments for the quantification of the study of arts and humanities have promised a scientification of those subjects, presenting this as an unambiguously good and unproblematic development. As Drucker has pointed out, some scholars mistakenly assume that these computational methods of analysis are objective, in contrast to 'the individuated and situated practices of human reading and interpretation'. She argues that: 'This objective fallacy is problematic. Designing a text-analysis program is necessarily an interpretative act, not a mechanical one, even if running the program becomes mechanistic' (Drucker, 2017: 634). This statement on text analysis can be applied more generally to digital methods as discussed in Chapter 4. As we argue further in the next chapter, quantitative measures only ever form part of the analysis of cultural artefacts and phenomena, and they function within a more complex set of intellectual manoeuvres.

The recent antipathy towards quantification has been caused in part by the fact that quantitative studies of arts and humanities data are not always undertaken by domain experts. As Ted Underwood has phrased it, 'Questions that historians and literary critics used to debate are increasingly scooped up by quantitative disciplines' (Underwood, 2019b), as in the now infamous 'culturomics' article written by a team led by evolutionary biologists in cooperation with Google, which analysed millions of digitised books and introduced the Ngram viewer to the world (Michel et al., 2011). The project was especially criticised for the lack of humanities expertise amongst its members. But scholars with a background in the arts and humanities who have chosen to employ quantitative measures have not been given an easier ride, as demonstrated by a number of prominent critiques in public forums (such as Stanley Fish's various outputs in the *New York Times*) and academic journals (such as Nan Z. Da's 2019 article in *Critical Inquiry*), and trace back many decades (such as Gutman's 1975 *Slavery and the Numbers Game*).

The point of this chapter, however, is not to examine the rhetoric surrounding quantification, but instead the rhetorical power of quantification itself. Numbers have the ability to capture certain attributes that cannot be gleaned simply by reading text or looking at images. Statistics can make an argument that cannot be expressed by words alone. Despite this, the quantitative is perceived as at odds with the normal practices and tropes of cultural commentary. Quantitative network analysis presents a challenge to traditional scholarship in the humanities not only in terms of methodology, but also in the ways in which we write about the findings from such a process. When faced with the graphs and statistics produced through the aforementioned processes, colleagues from more 'analogue' corners of the arts and humanities may struggle with the fundamental differences between these kinds of evidence and those typically presented in traditionally humanistic articles and monographs.

The tendency is to see these differences in terms of binary oppositions: the quantitative as opposed to the qualitative, numbers as opposed to words, graphs as opposed to text. This arises in part from the prevalent and enduring perception of the two cultures C. P. Snow described. His argument was that a central hindrance to solving many of the world's problems was the division of 'the intellectual life of the whole of western society' into what we call the sciences and the humanities (Snow, 1998: 3). Scholars in the field of digital humanities have tried to bridge those gaps, but their modes of expression have also been subject to critiques focusing on the binaries: in this case, close versus distant reading, interpretative versus descriptive work. Part III of this book argues that networks cut across those binaries. This chapter delves into the world of quantitative network analysis to show how the process of abstracting our objects of study into networks provides a way of quantifying culture, and examines the trade-offs we must consider to engage that kind of framework. Chapter 6 provides a set of practical manoeuvres for how to undertake that in the research and writing process.

The aim of this chapter is not to provide a tutorial on how to format data for off-the-shelf tools or for analysis with programming languages; dedicated tutorials do this in much more detail than we have space for here.[8] Our contention, rather, is that the use of any of these tools requires a prior *mental* manoeuvre of translating cultural artefacts into an abstracted form to see whether they are compatible with the input requirements of the available tools. This process of abstraction is not only a way of thinking, it also gives us algorithmic power. Certain kinds of networks are more compatible with existing quantitative approaches, and network analysis is simply inappropriate for some types of data. This does not necessarily have anything to do with the scale of the data. Although one of the arguments for quantitative approaches has been the complaint of too much data, there are also types of data that might be small but still need to be understood through abstract quantised description.

'Abstraction' can be an opaque term, but in essence it describes a deliberate reduction of the amount of available information. It is this 'information loss' on which critics of quantitative approaches have often focused in the humanities, but it is a much rarer critique in the field of network science, which takes the abstract network as its starting point. This information loss happens on a continuum. A greater level of abstraction generally means a greater number of available algorithms. In other words, to gain greater analytical power we must jettison more contextual information, at least temporarily. In the following pages, we illustrate this point using a toy example from the study of historical correspondence data that is nevertheless representative of the more general kinds of problems we face when deciding how to encode complex material and textual objects.

A letter can be considered to exist on (at least) three levels. The first is the material text: an object formed (normally) of paper or vellum, ink or pencil, seal or envelope, and marked by subsequent signs of filing. The

---

[8] For a thorough overview of tools and tutorials, see http://historicalnetworkre search.org/resources/external-resources/.

second, more abstract level is the letter contents, the textual matter. The final, most abstract level is the metadata level, as discussed in Chapter 3: here we are concerned with who wrote to whom and when, as well as further contextual information such as place of writing, document identifiers, etc. To make a letter network for quantitative analysis, all we really require in the first instance is the metadata level. Our toy example uses the following information:

- John Smith wrote to Peter Jones three times: on 3 January 1596, 21 March 1596, and 12 December 1597.
- Peter Jones wrote to John Smith once: on 4 February 1596.
- John Smith wrote to Mary Smith twice: on 15 May 1596 and 25 July 1597.

Writing about metadata might sound foreign to arts and humanities scholars. However, this list is not an unfamiliar way of encountering information about correspondence: we might summarise our research in this way in our notes or research outputs to provide an overview of a given person's or group's *oeuvre*. However, when we decide to structure this information as network data, we have a number of decisions to make.

We are assuming a model where the people are the nodes ('John Smith', 'Peter Jones', and 'Mary Smith'). Starting there, the question about abstraction therefore focuses on how to encode information about the letters that pass between them (the 'edges'), and which level of information to include when subjecting the network to mathematical measurements. We can visualise that decision process as outlined in Figure 13. Moving from left to right, we move across a landscape of abstraction, which entails more information loss the further we travel. The rightmost representation of the network merely records the existence of an edge between these nodes, without any attention to the time at which these edges formed, the direction in which letters travelled (who was the sender, who the recipient), or the volume of correspondence that travelled along those edges. One step less abstract is the *directed network*, which records the direction in which letters travelled (but not the volume), and the *weighted network*, which encodes the volume of correspondence that marks those edges (but not the direction). One further step leftward is the *weighted and directed network*, which combines the two previous network attributes, Finally, the leftmost

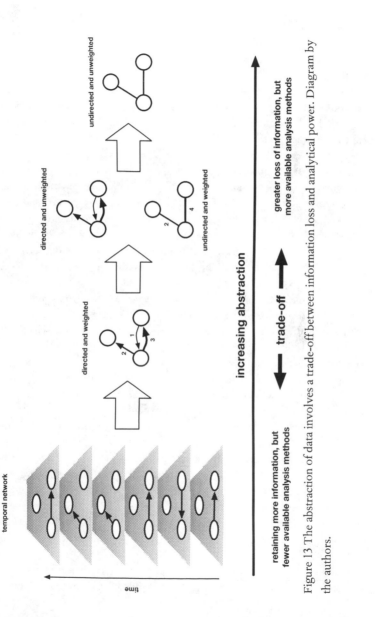

temporal network

directed and weighted

directed and unweighted

undirected and unweighted

undirected and weighted

increasing abstraction

trade-off

retaining more information, but
fewer available analysis methods

greater loss of information, but
more available analysis methods

time

Figure 13 The abstraction of data involves a trade-off between information loss and analytical power. Diagram by the authors.

network is a *temporal network*, which records the direction and time of every item of correspondence separately. None of these representations addresses the textual or material realities of a letter, either of which might be of critical importance to its understanding. The question is not whether metadata contains everything a historian might need, but under what circumstances the metadata by itself is still sufficient to reveal something historiographically notable and trustworthy.

So what trade-off is involved in working with that greatest level of abstraction? The right-most version of the network gives us the most algorithms with which we can analyse the network. This is because of the added challenge of designing a quantitative measurement for directed and weighted networks. As an example, we might consider the clustering coefficient, a metric for determining how densely the local neighbourhood of node is connected. This calculation takes the number of triangles (of edges) a node is involved in and divides it by the maximum number of possible triangles it could be part of if all neighbours were connected to each other. In an unweighted, undirected network, a triangle is easy to define, but in a directed network, we have seven different types of closed triangle due to the combinations of edge directions. In a weighted network, we have the added challenge of interpreting the weight quantitatively when the numerical value of the weight can mean very different things in different networks (e.g. a confidence score for an inferred interaction or a volume of correspondence flow between two individuals). Every retained layer of information therefore requires us to design a more complex quantitative measurement.

When faced with an unweighted, undirected network of correspondence, arts and humanities scholars are likely to balk at the amount of jettisoned information. Not only have we lost the material level and the contents of the letter – perhaps the most drastic step of coarse-graining in a correspondence network – but we have also dropped some elements of the metadata: the direction in which the letters are passing, how many letters there were, and the time-ordering of those letters. In this model, we are expressing an equivalence between a relationship marked by a single letter that is never reciprocated (e.g. a petition for release sent from a prisoner to a secretary of state that is ignored) and a reciprocal correspondence marked by hundreds of letters (e.g. a body of correspondence between that same secretary of state and his trusted diplomat). This is manifestly not true. But structurally many algorithms behave as if it is. Based on that, we might then assume that the solution is to push back leftward in the diagram in Figure 13 and to keep all the information about volume, weight, and temporal ordering. But the answer is not that simple: temporal networks are a subject of ongoing research in network science, and they are particularly challenging. Only very few network measurements can be generalised to temporal networks straightforwardly (Holme & Saramäki, 2013, 2019).

Where to locate oneself on the continuum of abstraction depends on the type of data used and on the research questions asked. Moreover, and as we argue in more detail in the following chapter, the research process will involve shifting back and forth across this continuum when addressing or honing a particular question. The best response to the trade-off between information loss and algorithmic power is to take advantage of both ends of the scale, manoeuvring between different registers of abstraction in order to work out where compromises can be made to get a preliminary result, which can then be confirmed, nuanced, and iterated upon with more tailored algorithmic combinations and a return to non-quantitative modes of humanistic inquiry. Here it might be useful to remember George E. P. Box's dictum: 'Essentially all models are wrong, but some are useful' (Box, 1979: 201–36).

What quantitative algorithms might then be useful to arts and humanities scholars? It is impossible to give an overview of them all, so the following is a quick glimpse of the possibilities some standard measures offer and of the way in which they were tailored to specific literary and historical research questions.[9]

An extremely simple network measure is a node's 'degree', which is the total number of connections it has with other nodes. For large data sets and social scientific problems, the distribution of degree values across all nodes in a network can be particularly revealing. Many varieties of observed networks across very different contexts display a highly skewed distribution of degrees. Barabási and Albert's foundational article, which we discussed in the introduction, showed that power grids, social networks, and the World Wide Web

---

[9] Other examples are discussed in the chapters on networks in Graham, Milligan, and Weingart (2015).

exhibit similar distributions (which can often be approximated by a power law, which is typically written as $P(k) \propto k^{\gamma}$, where k is the degree and γ is a constant). In all of these networks, a few nodes have many connections, more nodes have somewhat fewer connections, and a vast majority of nodes have very few connections. To give a very abstract example of such a network, we might have 1,000 nodes with degree 1, 100 nodes with degree 4, 10 nodes with degree 16, and 1 node with degree 64. At each level are ten times fewer nodes with four times as many connections. This relationship holds at every level of connectivity. The continuous nature of the scaling of these networks is the reason why they are also referred to as scale-free networks (Barabási & Albert, 1999).

But why are power laws in networks important? Weingart has made the point elsewhere that: 'The universe counts in powers rather than linear progressions, and thus in most cases a power law is not so much surprising as it is overwhelmingly expected. Reporting power laws in your data is a bit like reporting furry ears on your puppy' (Weingart, 2012). One way of using the power law distribution to think about more complex problems and to test theories can be found in the work of Pádraig Mac Carron and Ralph Kenna. They use the fact that power laws are an attribute of most observed social networks to investigate whether well-known myths (the *Iliad*, *Beowulf*, and the *Táin*) may have arisen from real historical events or are fictional. Most scholars believe the *Iliad* and *Beowulf* to be partly historical while the *Táin* is often considered entirely fictional. The network analysis, however, shows that all three myths have a (largely) scale-free degree distribution. By comparison, a control group of fictional texts contains no networks with this distribution, with the exception of one example for which part of the distribution exhibited scale-free characteristics (Harry Potter). More importantly, when plotting the distributions of the three myths side-by-side, one sees a striking similarity between the degree distributions of *Beowulf* and the *Táin* for all but the six most connected characters in the latter. This detail contributed to Carron and Kenna's contention that the perceived artificiality of the *Táin* network may be mainly associated with the corresponding six characters, and that this could have emerged through the gradual merging of characters during the oral transmission of the narrative (Carron & Kenna, 2012).

While the degree of a node is a fundamental measure for the analysis and comprehension of networks, it is also a fairly blunt instrument. However, numerous other 'centrality' measures use global properties of the network to help us understand the local significance of a node in interesting ways, such as closeness centrality, betweenness centrality, eigenvector centrality, and PageRank. As the name suggests, closeness centrality defines the centrality in terms of its distance to all other nodes. The peripherality of a node is defined as the sum of its distances from all other nodes; the 'closeness' is the inverse of this equation. Closeness can therefore be regarded as a measure of how long it will take to spread information from a given node to all other nodes sequentially. Linton Freeman first quantitatively defined betweenness centrality as the fraction of shortest paths between any two nodes in the network that passes through a given node or edge (Freeman, 1977).[10] For this reason, betweenness has been used to think quantitatively about the influence a node may have on the flow of information across the network. Following the emergence of large-scale computational network analysis, betweenness can now be calculated efficiently for large networks and can be used, for example, to find effective ways to fragment a network into disjoint components, and to identify modules, or 'communities' in the network. 'Eigenvector centrality' is closely related to the PageRank algorithm Google uses to assign importance to web pages on the World Wide Web and to rank its search results by relevance.[11] A node that has a high eigenvector score is one that is adjacent to nodes that are themselves high scorers. As Stephen Borgatti puts it, 'the idea is that even if a node influences just one other node, who subsequently influences many other nodes (who themselves influence still more others), then the first node in that chain is highly influential' (Borgatti, 2005: 61). These measurements require significant computing power and cannot be done by hand. The calculation of betweenness, for example, scales with the

---

[10] Although Freeman coined the term 'betweenness', very similar quantitative measures were suggested in studies before his, e.g. Pitts (1965).

[11] Once again, the PageRank algorithm has earlier predecessors, e.g. Pinski and Narin (1976), Saaty (1977).

cube of the number of nodes – if we increase the size of the network by a factor of ten, we require 1,000 times as much computer time.

It is important to realise that the decision to employ an algorithm also means that one is making a decision regarding the level of abstraction. Some algorithms were designed for directed edges, like PageRank, whereas other algorithms were, at least originally, designed for undirected edges, like most of the other centrality measures mentioned earlier. Some have several variants that can run on weighted or directed networks. In some cases, a weighted or directed version may have been proposed, but the implementation may be unfeasible in terms of computation time for a given network because it is too large. A smaller number of algorithms have been generalised to temporal networks, which are more challenging to analyse.

The question is whether the gain in computational power is worth the information loss. The answer depends on the research questions one is asking. Marten Düring's exploration of the 'reliability' of centrality measures for historical analysis draws attention both to the depth and complexity of humanities data, and the compromises and manoeuvres needed to flatten it sufficiently in order to render it suitable for centrality measures (Düring, 2016). His research seeks to reconstruct and understand the social process behind the helper networks that enabled Jews to survive the Holocaust, using data from survivor accounts and applications for reparation, amongst other sources. He sought to determine how good various centrality measures were at identifying individuals already judged significant by placing them in the top 10 per cent by that centrality measure. The ability of the measures to identify the known helpers varied significantly between the five networks and across the different measures employed: for example, across the five networks, betweenness identified as few as 25 per cent of individuals in one case, and 72 per cent in another; PageRank (not normally used in social networks) varied from 36 per cent to 90 per cent, and out-degree varied from 41 per cent to 81 per cent. Some of his networks seemed to yield better results from the centrality measures than others: for one particular network, 72–90 per cent of individuals were regarded as high ranking by all measures except eigenvector centrality. Düring tweaked the methods, trying to see if his influential figures were successfully 'discovered' if he expanded his search window to people placed in the top 20 per cent of scoring nodes using these measures. This was slightly more successful, with an average 70 per cent success rate, but a search window of this size is not necessarily that helpful if working on the scale of hundreds of thousands of actors.

This example demonstrates that single off-the-shelf algorithms, such as the centrality measures mentioned earlier, can provide useful first insights into the data, but the likelihood of any single measure being a reasonable proxy for the specific cultural attributes or phenomena one is looking for is minimal. To find the nodes or individuals of particular interest, or to develop more nuanced research questions beyond structural network questions, the measures typically need to be combined with other quantitative or qualitative approaches. For example, in their work on letter networks, Ruth and Sebastian Ahnert used combinations of measures to define a number of different categories of correspondents or of persons mentioned in letters. These combinations helped them to get closer to the historical features they were interested in than would have been possible with off-the-shelf metrics. No amount of fiddling with measurements is going to offer you a one-to-one equivalence with your object of inquiry. In humanistic network analysis, the objective should not be to exactly map the size of the territory; we are merely seeking metrics that will act as useful prosthetic to our own process of humanistic inquiry, itself never perfect.

Ruth and Sebastian Ahnert's first attempt at creating network 'profiles' of figures was demonstrated in their article on Protestant letter networks in the reign of Mary I, which used epistolary data to explore how an underground community that spread across England and onto the continent was managed during a period of intense persecution (Ahnert & Ahnert, 2015). By creating thresholds for five network measures and labelling values for these measures as high or low, they were able to provide predictions about whether a node was one of three categories of 'leader', three categories of network 'sustainer' (including financial supporters and letter couriers), or a peripheral figure.[12] These predictions were largely accurate and enabled

---

[12] The measures were: betweenness, eigenvector centrality, letter degree (the number of senders and recipients connected to a node), letter strength (the total number of letters received and sent by a given node), and non-letter social degree (how many links they had to other nodes via means other than the sending or receiving of a letter).

them to see general trends in the patterns of communication within the Protestant community. For example, by looking at how the different categories of nodes interacted, they observed that the most prolific leaders frequently and repeatedly wrote to network sustainers, meaning that the shortest paths across the network were also the ones most frequently traversed by letters and, by implication, carriers.

Categories of people such as those defined for the Protestant network show how network analysis enables us to manoeuvre between different registers of quantitative analysis, from micro, to meso, to macro. Both the use of centrality measures and the construction of network 'profiles' are about generating a quantitative description of certain attributes of a single node as a function of their position *in the entire network*. Centrality measures can also be used to think about the mesoscopic properties of complex networks. For example, the discovery that an easy way to fragment a network is to target nodes or edges with the highest betweenness (Holme et al., 2002) explains the effectivity of betweenness-based community detection algorithms such as the Newman–Girvan algorithm. This is because high betweenness nodes and edges often act as bridges between different regions of a network, and so the idea is that removing them will help reveal the make-up of different regions or communities. Although the evaluation of the effectiveness of the various algorithms to detect community structure is still an open question, such algorithms might be adopted to think about communities beyond the literal social dimension, such as 'communities' of literary features of artistic motifs.

Our discussion has only scratched the surface of the kinds of quantitative analysis that can be applied to cultural data. But how attainable are these kinds of analysis to humanities researchers? Calling on arts and humanities researchers to employ quantitative methods or offering a tantalising glimpse of their potential is pointless if they are not reasonably within reach. This brings us to a cost of the application of quantitative measures. To move confidently around the abstract realm of statistics and algorithms requires certain skills or tools.

The humanities scholar interested in quantitative and visual methods for network analysis has an increasing number of tools at their disposal. These range from out-of-the-box software for visualisation such as Palladio or

Gephi, mentioned in the previous chapter, to much more involved tools such as the NetworkX Python library.[13] The level of technological sophistication is primarily an issue of access, not of the research problem. In principle, it is preferable to choose the most advanced method available, as the more advanced methods can do everything the more basic methods can, with more ability to customise approaches and run more complex analysis. In practice, however, the advanced methods require an investment of time either to learn them or to find a suitable collaborator. And as it may not be clear from the beginning whether quantitative methods will be useful in a particular research context, it can be helpful to use the more basic tools to get a sense of the utility of a quantitative approach before spending time and energy on more refined analysis techniques. The investment required to gain skills in new software, programming languages, and libraries may then yield academic returns on those investments, but those returns of course are determined not only by the results arrived at, but also by the value attributed to that kind of work within our academic structures.

As discussed in Chapter 4, Tommaso Venturini, Mathieu Jacomy, and Pablo Jensen have argued that one of the values of out-of-the-box tools is that they provide a way of gaining a quantitative vocabulary that opens communication with other disciplines (Venturini et al., 2019). This in turn may lower the bar for taking digital humanities courses or participating in summer schools which can teach how to code and use advanced visualisation packages. For those without the time to make that leap, familiarity with out-of-the-box software can provide a level of fluency in the language of networks that makes it easier to find collaborators. But we would warn against using such tools without doing background reading or undertaking additional training. Ultimately the mastery of the quantitative approach by the humanities scholars themselves promises the greatest amount of control and depth of understanding, but the highest level of time investment. One of the risks to using off-the-shelf tools is the black-box effect: you input data and get results without fully understanding the algorithms through which those results were generated.

---

[13] In programming, a library is a collection of precompiled routines a program can use.

A further point needs to be made here: within the current educational context, individuals who have all the requisite skills to engage in cultural analysis in rigorous quantitative ways are a rare breed. That combination of skills tends to point to an atypical educational or professional route, or somebody who has sought out extra training. In light of the changing ways in which culture is studied, we contend that a pressing duty is placed on the university to prepare future generations of academics by offering suitable combinations of courses in humanities subjects, programming, and statistical methods. This is not simply to say that humanities scholars need to be trained to be statistically savvy, but that students entering STEM pathways need to also be alert to the complexity and interest of arts and humanities data and to the critical skills those disciplines provide. But the barriers to this are not just presented at the level of the university curriculum or departmental structures; rather, they are also a manifestation of the choices students are forced to make at a much earlier stage in their educational lives. In the UK, for example, humanities students at university could have dropped all STEM subjects at the age of sixteen. There are more subtle, but significant factors that funnel students from European or North American schools into mutually exclusive science or humanities pathways. All might be described as manifestations of the two cultures problem. Until such massive structural changes are addressed (if they can be), we need to think practically about how to bridge the quantitative and qualitative spheres, working with the system and the expertise that we have and gaining additional skills and experience where we can.

The other way of bringing together those diverse skills, as we have already demonstrated by co-authoring this book, is through collaboration. As a team of writers, we encapsulate a range of ways into studying cultural networks and a range of different skills and areas of expertise, including English literature and book history, history of science and informatics, information design, and physics and complex networks. The large majority of our work on networks has been done in collaboration. But collaborative work is not straightforward, especially when bridging disciplines. Interdisciplinary collaborations bring together people from different research backgrounds with their respective modes of working, publishing, and sharing credit and data. In order to work together effectively, all collaborators need to be prepared for an ongoing dialogue, revision of each other's assumptions and research questions, and a willingness to engage iteratively with the research methods, disciplinary language, and research questions of the other partners. All partners need to be committed to building shared understanding, which necessarily means gaining new knowledge and moving away from one's assumptions about how things are done.

One of the benefits of a collaboration between scholars in the humanities and sciences is that it forces them to confront assumptions about their research methods and how their research will enter the world. As part of the Elements 'Gathering' on Digital Literary Culture, we want to be self-reflexive about the fact that this is a multi-authored book. For us, this is an important statement of the way network analysis sits at the intersection of science, humanities, and design practices. But seeing four authors on the cover of a book is also meant to be a provocation in and of itself. In the sciences, collaborative research and multi-authored publications are the norm. In certain scientific subfields, there are established ways of ordering the authors' names to reflect the contributions of individual authors, as well as their seniority. In the humanities, we lack these norms because the practice of having more than two authors remains relatively rare. In this book, we have decided to list authors alphabetically, but our colleagues in the arts and humanities might want to consider other options if and when the practice becomes more standard, such as Debraj Ray and Arthur Robson's proposal for random author ordering, which was presented in response to the argument that alphabetical ordering is discriminatory (Ray & Robson, 2018). The American Economic Association now permits this practice.

This decision to co-author a book also presents an ethical provocation. The kinds of projects being encouraged and funded in the arts and humanities are increasingly digital and collaborative and involve the labour of both junior academic colleagues and technical colleagues outside formal academic tracks. We therefore need to be increasingly aware of the way we credit labour. There are countless examples of work that is the product of a whole team's efforts but is attributed to a sole author who thanks the other members of the team in a footnote or the acknowledgements. This requires a change in culture in a number of places, most notably within higher education institutions and in particular in the way they evaluate the evidence in support of tenure and promotion applications and the credit they give to co-publication. But arts and humanities publishers also have a powerful part to play by welcoming multi-authored works and accommodating non-standard content, including formulas, graphs, and network diagrams. If leading university presses support this work, then promotion and tenure committees will be forced to consider it too.

The quantification of culture can therefore play an active part in challenging the model of single authorship in the arts and humanities. The question that follows, however, is how we can produce scholarship that is accessible to audiences from all the contributing disciplines. In constructing practices of research that lie at the intersection of several disciplines, we need to make sure that we have created something greater than the sum of its parts, rather than something lesser, such as an interdisciplinary silo in which we are only speaking to other displaced scholars. Rather, as we argue in Chapter 6, the network perspective enables a set of manoeuvres that draw together different disciplinary practices and norms into an iterative process.

6 Networking the 'Divided Kingdom'

While quantitative approaches to the arts and humanities have their propo-
nents, a mistrust of this kind of work remains in many corners of the arts and
humanities. The reasons are complex and tied up with attempts to defend
disciplines in the face of shrinking student numbers and shifts in funding
patterns, which seem to be diverting money to digital projects that had
previously been allotted to more traditional humanistic endeavours. What
is particularly interesting, however, is the way that written defences of the
humanities often construct their arguments on the assumption of bounded
disciplinary territories, which (either implicitly or explicitly) set up binary
oppositions between the 'scientific' and 'humanistic' modes of inquiry. Neo-
Kantian philosopher Wilhelm Windelband has described the differences in
style of argumentation between the sciences and humanities as 'nomothetic
versus idiographic'. Windelband argues that the nomothetic is typical of
scientific disciplines, which have a tendency towards methods and approaches
designed to derive generalisable laws to explain categories of phenomena. By
contrast, scholarship in the arts and humanities is more comfortable with what
Windelband calls the idiographic, the tendency to specify what is contingent,
unique, or subjective (Caviglia & Coleman, 2016; Weingart, 2014b). But our
argument is that a well-designed network approach to cultural data reorients
us in such a way that those binaries are eradicated. This is not to say that
networks solve the issue of the two cultures. But the moment of consilience
that brought us to this network turn shows that the network perspective does
not belong to one field. It decouples the object of study from methodological
approaches in a way that provides a model for research that seeks to transcend
traditional disciplinary norms.

Michael Witmore draws attention to the territorial metaphors of disciplinary gatekeeping in his article on 'Latour, the Digital Humanities, and the
Divided Kingdom of Knowledge'. Setting up the two imagined kingdoms of
scientific and humanistic inquiry, his article sets out to challenge the perception
within the humanities of a hostile incursion of scientific method. Leaning on
Latour, he writes: 'What humanists are trying to save (that is, reflexive inquiry
directed at artifacts) was never a distinct form of knowledge. It is a province
without borders, one that may be impossible to defend' (Witmore, 2016: 353).

Witmore's ventriloquisation of the humanist's concerns that digital methods 'have strayed into our province from the sciences' and of the need to establish 'countermeasures' to deflect 'incursions across battle lines' moves swiftly from territorialism to outright war over that territory. What is particularly interesting about the attitude Witmore is pushing against is the conflation of the object of study ('artefacts') and the methods of analysis ('reflexive inquiry') in that territory. The implication inherent in the body of literature seeking to 'defend' the arts and humanities is that certain objects of study are necessarily tied to a certain set of methodological approaches.

The territorial metaphor interestingly occurs again in an important study on collaboration in the sciences which a number of digital humanities scholars have cited (e.g. Svensson, 2012). Peter Galison employed the metaphor of a 'trading zone' to explain how physicists from different paradigms went about collaborating with each other and with engineers to develop particle detectors and radar. His experience of working in different laboratories revealed a division of scientific cultures that exemplifies a kind of fractal of the greater fissure identified by C. P. Snow. The metaphor of the trading zone adapts anthropological studies of the development of pidgin languages and creoles in border zones to allow communication and the exchange of goods. According to Galison:

> Two groups can agree on rules of exchange even if they ascribe utterly different significance to the objects being exchanged; they may even disagree on the meaning of the exchange process itself. Nonetheless, the trading partners can hammer out a local coordination, despite vast global differences. In an even more sophisticated way, cultures in interaction frequently establish contact languages, systems of discourse that can vary from the most function-specific jargons, through semi-specific pidgins, to full-fledged creoles rich enough to support activities as complex as poetry and metalinguistic reflection. (Galison, 1997: 783)

Galison's is a hugely valuable model for how collaborations can arise and evolve into something beneficial to all the parties involved. Galison and those working in his wake have developed the idea to explain how such trading zones can gradually become a new area of expertise in their own right, facilitated by people who have developed a specific kind of 'interactional expertise', a fluency in that creole (Gorman, 2010).

Networks require interactional expertise. But the intellectual and methodological manoeuvres that underpin a network approach to culture render the metaphor of territory and border inadequate. Even if we allow the idea of new emerging geographies of scholarship, the metaphor still ties certain practices to certain territories in the mind. However, as the foregoing chapters have sought to demonstrate, the network perspective does not belong to any particular territory. Rather it is a set of approaches we can bring to almost any object of study. As such it forces us to mentally reorient ourselves in relation to that powerful metaphor, rotating ourselves by 90 degrees to any territory, whether that be nineteenth-century newspapers or a common artistic motif replicated in print. Our contention is that the manoeuvres of the network approach move us not across that land mass but rather perpendicular to it, shifting our distance from it to take different yet complementary views on our object of study in order to build a fuller, iterative mode of analysis. As such we proffer an alternative metaphor of the aerial photograph and its utility in archaeology, one that decouples the method from the object of study.

As a new technology compared to the discipline of archaeology, aerial photography has acted to complement and extend the more traditional research practice of archaeological fieldwork. The aerial photograph sacrifices resolution and detail in return for the ability to spot large-scale patterns and discover previously overlooked features. But the photo is necessarily part of an iterative research process: the plane taking aerial photographs is employed in a region that is of interest to researchers on the ground. Depending on the research at hand, a particular altitude (or level of coarse-graining) and a particular type of imaging technology (akin to the choice of quantitative analysis algorithm) are chosen. Mapping technologies therefore recall the kinds of trade-off discussed in the previous chapter between scale and precision and the affordances they offer for the task at hand: you can measure the length of a shoreline only from a distance; up close, it is a fractal of sand and water of infinite length. Features recorded in the aerial photograph can then be investigated on the ground, for example in the form of an archaeological excavation where vegetation patterns imply buried foundations. The findings of that examination on the ground can then inform further rounds of aerial photography, perhaps in other regions or with other imaging techniques – perhaps ones that are more sensitive to the features of interest on the ground.

Aerial archaeology has enabled the discovery of hundreds of previously unknown archaeological sites, but it has also helped to make sense of known, clearly visible prehistoric landscape features, such as the Nazca Lines in Peru, which form a large-scale pattern that makes sense only when viewed from a great height. More recently, this approach has been extended to satellite photography and to remote sensing from space. Like aerial photographs, quantitative approaches in the arts and humanities do not seek to replace other methods, but to provide a powerful complementary approach that can facilitate the discovery of specific new case studies as well as give rise to a vantage point from which local features merge into a more meaningful large-scale pattern. The network perspective reveals different things to the scholar at different scales, and so it is vital to make use of that full scalar range of analysis in order to rigorously analyse the particular territory under scrutiny. We connect this metaphor to three broad levels of analysis: the satellite view (macro), the aerial view (meso), and the archaeological dig (micro), although of course there are gradations (and, indeed, fractals) within these too.

These levels and the movement between them are not only descriptive of a research process; they also provide a way of thinking about the different kinds of arguments that can be put forward and the most suitable kinds of venues in which to share those. The satellite view should not be understood as an 'angelic' perspective which assumes a particular privileged vantage point of the observer and a firm and consistent reality of the observed. Rather, it is one of multiple views that form part of a heuristic process requiring the scholar to move through a whole set of perspectives both to validate and problematise what is seen from the other vantage points. The necessity of a shifting scale of analysis has been persuasively and repeatedly argued for by digital humanities scholars like Ted Underwood, who has written that 'literary history cannot spend all of its time thirty thousand feet above the ground' (Underwood, 2019a: xxi). However, more thought is still needed about how and when to make those shifts and the implications for how we write and publish this kind of work.

First we might think about these scales as stages of a research process, by looking at a worked example that moves from a coarse-grained satellite picture to more local aerial observations, then an archaeological dig in the archive, and finally an iterative step to the development of a more nuanced process for understanding local commonalities. The example is from Ruth and Sebastian Ahnert's work on the 132,747 letters in the Tudor State Papers archive (Ahnert & Ahnert, 2019). To begin with, they gained a coarse-grained overview of the archive by measuring the degree of all the people in the correspondence network (see Chapter 5), which provided the distribution of the number of correspondents each person had. The result was a clear power law distribution: while ~68 per cent of people in the network had a degree of just 1 (meaning they corresponded with a single person), one person had a total degree of 4,405. However, as discussed earlier, proving that a network has a scale-free degree distribution is relatively uninteresting, but by comparing the degree of each correspondent with their betweenness centrality ranking, they found a way to distinguish the 'bridges' from the hubs in the network and thus to identify people fulfilling particular infrastructural roles. A graph of these two measures for each decade of data reveals a strong correlation between the measures, resulting in a clear diagonal line: in other words, the more correspondents a person has, the higher their betweenness is (i.e. the number of short paths that passed through them). However, in all decades are outliers from the trend line with higher betweenness and lower degree (Figure 14 shows this graph for the 1580s). They focused on this region of the graphs in order to understand local commonalities (leading to the local aerial view).

Here it is important to pause and to note the important role visualisation plays in the identification of global and local patterns. To think about the close relationship between quantitative results and visualisation, we might consider the different layers of a geographical map, such as those available in Google Maps. In this now ubiquitous interface, we toggle between satellite, map, and street views because of the different things they can show us. Similarly, in a research process using network metrics, we might move from tables of quantitative results to various ways of plotting those numbers that are more visually intuitive or revealing. It was only through visualisation (the graph) that Ruth and Sebastian Ahnert discovered the outliers. What they

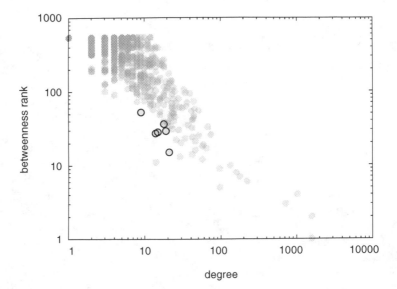

Figure 14 Betweenness rank versus degree for the correspondence network of the 1580s, derived from the Tudor State Papers. The six highlighted individuals (black rings) with relatively low degree and relatively high betweenness are Catholic conspirators. Note that degree increases to the right and betweenness increases downwards due to use of betweenness rank rather than raw score (which is expressed as a fraction). Diagram by the authors.

saw through further investigation into the identities of those outliers was that from the 1570s onward, a large number of the people in that region of the graph were Catholic conspirators involved in plots against Elizabeth I and double agents gathering information on those plotters for the Tudor government (see Figure 14). However, to understand why that pattern was emerging, they needed to get much closer to the ground, digging into the individual letters, to understand why conspirators and spies might have this particular combination of network attributes. This excavation confirmed that although such figures correspond with a relatively small number of people, they were making contact between otherwise separate communities – and in the case of double agents, radically opposed communities.

The archaeological dig into the letters in turn occasioned another iteration: the discovery that certain kinds of writers exhibited certain combinations of higher or lower network measurements led to the development of a more sophisticated method to find 'similar' people in the network. By taking an array of eight different network measurements, they developed a way of placing individuals in a multidimensional space in which the spatial distance between two people signifies their similarity in terms of network measurements. The groupings of people that arise from this algorithm can then be investigated (once again) through close reading, which reveals that this abstract approach does surprisingly well. For example, of the fifteen people most similar to the exiled Catholic conspirator William Allen, thirteen were also Catholic men perceived to present foreign threats to England's security. Another example is Pietro Bizzarri, who was an 'intelligencer' (a contemporary word for a person who gathers intelligence, like a spy or secret agent) for the Tudor government based in Venice from 1564. Of the fifteen people with the most similar network profile, fourteen were also intelligencers, but their formal roles varied widely and included military leaders, diplomatic servants, and merchants; what they all had in common was the regular pattern of information they sent to the Tudor government. Quantitative methods can therefore reveal commonalities that might otherwise be hard to see and offer new ways of understanding the histories of organisations and communities.

The correlative to the scales of investigation – the satellite view, the aerial view, and the archaeological dig – are the different kinds of argument that can be proffered. While a fruitful application of network analysis in the humanities almost certainly will contain all three registers of analysis in order to verify findings and iterate better methods, we might still choose to conduct our narrative in one dominant mode. This has implications for where we choose to publish our work. An argument that sits predominantly in the satellite mode might concern fundamental changes in the power structure of a government across decades, the emergence of whole genres in literature, or the differences between the character networks of hundreds of playwrights across centuries. Such was the motivation of the field of cliometrics (new economic history), which emerged in the late 1950s and early 1960s but had all but disappeared from anglophone history departments by the 1980s due in part to the controversy surrounding the claims about American slavery by Robert Fogel and Stanley Engerman in *Time on the Cross* (Fogel & Engerman, 1974). Fogel and Engerman argued that their economic models revealed that previous histories of American slavery, which contended that the practice was economically inefficient and only maintained for reasons of custom and prestige, were wrong and that the practice was, in fact, also profitable for the South. As well as charges of an ideological agenda and qualitative decontextualisation, the research was subsequently revealed to be built on biased samples, errors, and numerous exaggerations, which brought not only the authors into disrepute, but the entire field of cliometrics (see Boldizzoni, 2011: 15–17). More recently, Jo Guldi and David Armitage in their *History Manifesto* have called for a return to quantitative methods and longue durée history in response to the availability of data at scale (Guldi & Armitage, 2014); their call was met with a surprisingly fierce backlash. Quantitative approaches promise and deliver some of the most fundamental and challenging findings, which leaves them open to warranted and unwarranted controversy.

The controversy derives in part from the fact that in the arts and humanities, contributions to the field of knowledge tend to be incremental, detailed, grounded, and alert to local inconsistencies, ambiguities, and subjective experience. The challenge then is how to connect satellite-level arguments to a history of scholarship on a subject that is pieced together from archaeological excavation. Some may argue that this connection is not essential; that such results are part of an emergent, parallel form of humanities scholarship, the value of which will be accepted in time. The real risk is that the two forms of the discipline stay parallel, publishing, educating, and thus propagating separately. The entrenchment that may result would damage both sides if the continuum of scale discussed earlier becomes an artificial dichotomy that leads the traditional community to reject even lower-level, uncontroversial quantitative approaches, and the digital community to place less value on quantitative work that does not operate at the largest scales.

A similar problem is found with arguments made at the scale of the local aerial view, where we might use combinations of quantitative methods and visualisation to define commonalities or relationships between the entities studied. In the network context, this could be an attempt to classify the roles of individuals in a correspondence network as discussed earlier, the categorisation of characters in plays, or shared motifs in illustrations. Such an approach is therefore prone to critiques that identify exceptions, thereby making generalisable rules seem reductionist and raising questions about the validity of such approaches. Concerns of this nature can be addressed by ensuring that the conclusions drawn from such generalisations remain connected to existing scholarship on the objects of study. But with the increasing scale of that generalisation, the maintenance of that connection requires an increasing amount of labour and care.

One suggested way to overcome the considerable gap between established scholarship and quantitative approaches on the largest scale is to demand falsifiable models of the scientific kind. The call for reproducible research has recently been amplified in the humanities by the 2019 Da article. There are good reasons for resisting some of the recommendations Da makes to editors to ensure reproducibility because of the huge and unrealistic burden they place on individual researchers, in ways that hold them to standards much higher than those we see in other disciplines across the sciences as well as in the humanities. Nevertheless, it is important to acknowledge that if findings become reproducible across different domains of knowledge, they also potentially become more valuable. For example, if the quantitative evidence for the emergence of a particular genre shows a pattern that is subsequently found to underlie the emergence of other genres or categories of texts in other literary contexts, then that pattern becomes much more meaningful. Similarly, if a transition in the power structure of a government network shares properties with other such transitions in other periods, those properties become much more significant. But those interested in generalisable models are unlikely to be those interested in the particular systems being analysed, such as the example given earlier of categories of correspondent in an early modern epistolary archive. To complicate matters further, the perspectival nature of much of humanities research fundamentally resists the concept of replication, embracing uniqueness and ungeneralisability in the idiographic tradition. We contend that when scholarship can be reproducible or reusable, it should be, but scholarship that cannot fit in that mould should not be forced into it.

The final scale of research output is that which corresponds to the archaeological dig. In this case we are using the metaphor to denote the way quantitative analysis can help to discover the overlooked example of a known kind, or an anomaly or outlier that may form the basis for a case study of interest. In the analogy of aerial archaeology, this might be the remnants of an individual building that is discovered from above due to markings in a field. This application is without doubt a valuable use of quantitative approaches in the age of large digital archives that nobody can close-read in their entirety. It is a use that is close to traditional methods, one step up from the search box on the digital archive website, and thus largely uncontroversial. We might find such an example by graphing data, as in Figure 14, and finding amongst the epistolary outliers – in this case the conspirators and double agents – a figure who has received no scholarly attention. That alone does not make him or her worthy of study, but if that figure can be used to prove the effectiveness of a method (e.g. for discovering spies and conspirators) or to illustrate a general trend in the epistolary habits of such figures, then they might become the focus of an article or even a book-length study.

Implicit in the descriptions cited earlier is the idea that certain scales of argument tend to belong in certain publication venues. Although network analysis encourages a set of manoeuvres and scalar shifts that breaks away from both the methods and modes of argumentation associated with specific disciplinary norms, the publishing landscape follows the more territorial structure from which we sought to distinguish ourselves earlier in this book. Digital humanities journals and book series provide one option, and increasing numbers of publication venues aim at interdisciplinary work. We applaud those especially that are thinking outside the boxes of standard publication formats, such as Stanford Digital Projects and Minnesota University Press's projects hosted on the Manifold platform. These might be the best venue for reaching like-minded readers who seek to push the boundaries of new methods and approaches for studying culture.

There are, however, a number of arguments to be made for framing our work in ways tailored to journals and book series in our home disciplines. From an ideological perspective, this is the best way to expand the community of scholars working on cultural network analysis. By showing our colleagues in departments across the arts and humanities that networks offer approaches and insights useful to them, we extend the number of allies we have with whom we can develop and extend the methods and discourse of networks in ways that meet the needs of humanistic inquiry. On the other hand, by working with our scientific collaborators to publish in venues favoured by colleagues in their fields, we can show that our cultural artefacts provide data that presents exciting new challenges and opportunities to develop new computational approaches and to question the applicability and subtlety of those currently in use. But there is also a practical argument to be made: for promotion and tenure, we need to demonstrate to colleagues and committees that we can place our work in venues *known* to be esteemed. But to get them accepted into such venues is a two-part challenge. First, we need to find editors willing to take a risk on something that is unfamiliar. Second, we need to continue developing ways of writing that look enough like the kind of scholarship one normally sees in those venues to be accessible, but that introduce new methods, specialist language, and modes of argumentation that push the reader beyond their comfort zone. Only by doing this can we change what our home disciplines regard as the methodologies that belong to their objects of study. This is how we change perspectives.

Epilogue

We did not want to finish this book with a 'conclusion' because of the connotations of a decisive judgement and closure. Rather than having the final word, we wish to start a conversation; instead of closing we wish instead to proffer an opening. This was one of the key reasons we chose to publish open access – so that this book would be available to anyone who wished to engage with it, and so that it could be set in classrooms and reading groups as a prompt for critical response. To create this opening, therefore, we wish to offer a set of invitations.

We invite our colleagues in the arts and humanities who have not yet succumbed to the network turn to explore whether it might offer you a method or critical framework, to read some of the scholarship cited earlier, to play with one of the out-of-the-box network visualisation tools, to sign up to a training event. We invite you to feel that you have the critical acumen to meaningfully engage with the network turn even if you do not feel like you have the technical expertise (yet). It is an invitation to have a conversation with colleagues in other departments and disciplines who may have been working with network analysis for a while, an invitation to try a small collaborative project.

We invite our colleagues in the natural and computational sciences to reach out to colleagues in the arts and humanities who might have data or research questions that will challenge you in new ways. We invite you to enter into collaboration not as a colleague with a solution, but rather with a commitment to ongoing conversation and iterative development, to learn about the fields with which you are partnering and from their critical frameworks. Through these partnerships, we invite you to question your current assumptions about the gathering, processing, and analysis of data: what is 'clean' enough, how you encode incompleteness and uncertainty and how you account for biases at each stage of the data pipeline, from the collection process, to the blind spots of existing algorithms, to the way we interpret our results.

We invite scholars of all disciplinary backgrounds to make sure you include software and interface designers and visualisation specialists in your projects and collaborations as key team members, and not merely as service providers. And we invite designers to think critically about how interfaces, tools, and visualisations are positioned within a long and iterative research process; to design with an eye to discovery, knowledge creation, and disruption; to avoid smoothing away uncertainty and absence, but rather draw the eyes of the user and, by implication, the terms of the critical debate to those issues.

We invite editors to consider articles and book proposals that might seem to differ in style and content from their usual fare. Editors of arts and humanities journals and series, we invite you to embrace publications with quantitative results, tables, graphs, and visualisations that form a part of their arguments; to work with your authors to help polish a style that will engage the current readership, but also challenge them productively. Those of you working in the natural and computational sciences, we invite you to consider seriously the importance of articles working with cultural data to break new ground methodologically and critically.

Finally, we invite our universities to facilitate this work by creating opportunities and space to develop inter- and cross-disciplinary conversations, to support and reward those at all career stages who take risks by thinking outside the norms of their fields to develop new or unfamiliar ways of working. We suggest that the onus should not be placed on individual researchers to create these connections; rather, strategic changes need to be made to the education of our students to ensure future generations are equipped to tackle the practical and academic challenges of our digital world. In the networked world, an education that does not bring together humanistic, artistic, scientific, and technical training is incomplete.

The optimism of these invitations, however, must be considered alongside the pressing need for critical engagement with the threats posed to privacy and security by the network turn. We are all aware of the ways in which companies and governments can exploit network data and advanced network analysis for the purposes of power, surveillance, and commercial gain. We might think of the sobering words of Alex Younger, the chief of the Secret Intelligence Service (MI6) in the UK, that 'The connectivity that is the heart of globalisation can be exploited by states with hostile intent to further their aims ... The risks at stake are profound and represent a fundamental threat to our sovereignty' (King, 2017). As technology changes apace, the legal frameworks that govern the uses and abuses of data are struggling to keep up.

The study and (minimal) critique of networks in the public eye has unsurprisingly been dominated by voices from the sciences, the technology sector, and the military-industrial complex. These communities, after all, built the proximate causes of the network turn. But as Part I of this book shows, their way was paved by deep cultural forces, and the network turn's echo will reverberate in every corner of society for years to come. All those whose work touches on the relationships between structure and society will need to work together to understand the implications of the network turn and intervene when necessary. As scholars, designers, librarians, archivists, scientists, and other practitioners of network analysis, we need to invite ourselves to speak truth to power: to advise, warn, and lead by example. It is tempting to retreat into the safe spaces of curiosity-driven research, but we are also compelled to engage with industry and the government's advisory bodies, to agitate for the values and best practices we seek to develop. Of course, many of these spheres are closed to ordinary researchers. Indeed, we have good evidence that those spaces where practices are most ethically troubling are the most closely guarded. But we must find ways in. We must situate ourselves within the broader economy of knowledge in which we are working, to understand how the methods we are developing and the data we are generating can be co-opted. And where other options are closed to us, we might look to the example of Lombardi: to take up the tools available to us and to draw out those systems that need scrutiny for all to see.

Bibliography

Abbot, A. (2014). Humanity's cultural history captured in 5-minute film. *Nature News*, 31 July. Available at: www.nature.com/news/humanity-s-cultural-history-captured-in-5-minute-film-1.15650.

Adamic, L., Lento, T., Adar, E., & Ng, P. C. (2016). Information evolution in social networks. *Proceedings of the Ninth ACM International Conference on Web Search and Data Mining*, 473–82.

Ahn, Y., Ahnert, S. E., Bagrow, J. P., & Barabási, A. (2011). Flavor network and the principles of food pairing. *Scientific Reports*, 1, article 196.

Ahnert, R. & Ahnert, S. E. (2015). Protestant letter networks in the reign of Mary I: A quantitative approach. *English Literary History*, 82, 1–33.

(2019). Metadata, surveillance and the Tudor state. *History Workshop Journal*, 87, 27–51.

(forthcoming). *Tudor Networks of Power*. Oxford: Oxford University Press.

Ariew, R. (1992). Descartes and the Tree of Knowledge. *Synthese*, 92, 101–16.

Bacon, F. (1640). *Of the Advancement and Proficiencie of Learning, or, The Partitions of Sciences, IX Bookes*. Oxford: Printed by Leon Lichfield printer to the University, for Robert Young and Edward Forrest.

Ball, J., Borger, J., & Greenwald, G. (2013). Revealed: How US and UK spy agencies defeat internet privacy and security. *Guardian*, 6 September. Available at: www.theguardian.com/world/2013/sep/05/nsa-gchq-encryption-codes-security.

Barabási, A. (2002). *Linked: The New Science of Networks*. Cambridge, MA: Perseus.

Barabási, A. & Albert, R. (1999). Emergence of scaling in random networks. *Science*, 286, 5439.

Bastian, M., Heymann, S., & Jacomy, M. (2009). Gephi: An open source software for exploring and manipulating networks. *Proceedings of the Third International ICWSM Conference*, 361–2.

Boldizzoni, F. (2011). *The Poverty of Clio: Resurrecting Economic History*. Princeton, NJ: Princeton University Press.

Borgatti, S. P. (2005). Centrality and network flow. *Social Networks*, 27, 55–71.

Box, G. E. P. (1979). Robustness in the strategy of scientific model building. In R. L. Launer & G. N. Wilkinson, eds., *Robustness in Statistics*. New York: Academic Press, 5.1.

Broido, A. D. & Clauset, A. (2019). Scale-free networks are rare. *Nature Communications*, 10, 1017.

Buurma, R. S. & Heffernan, L. (2018). Search and replace: Josephine Miles and the origins of distant reading. *Modernism/modernity*, 3(1). Available at: https://modernismmodernity.org/forums/posts/search-and-replace.

Callon, M. (1984). Some elements of a sociology of translation: Domestication of the scallops and the fishermen of St Brieuc Bay. *Sociological Review*, 32, 196–233.

Caviglia, G. & Coleman, N. (2016). Idiographic network visualisations. *Leonardo*, 49(5), 447–447.

Coleman, C. N. (2020). Seeking the eye of history: The design of digital tools for Enlightenment studies. In S. Burrows & G. Roe, eds., *Digitizing Enlightenment: Digital Humanities and the Transformation of Eighteenth-Century Studies*. Oxford University Studies in the Enlightenment. Liverpool: Liverpool University Press,

Coleridge, S. T. (1817). *Lay Sermon Addressed to the Higher and Middle Classes on the Existing Distresses and Discontents*. London: Printed for Gale and Fenner.

Da, N. Z. (2019). The computational case against computational literary studies. *Critical Inquiry*, 45, 601–39.

Daston, L. J. (2008). On scientific observation. *Isis*, 99, 97–110.

Deleuze, G. & Guattari, F. (1980). *Capitalisme et Schizophrénie 2. Mille Plateaux*.Paris: Minuit.

Diminescu, D. (2012). Introduction: Digital methods for the exploration, analysis and mapping of e-diasporas. *Social Science Information*, 51(4), 451–8.

Drucker, J. (2011). Humanities approaches to graphical display. *Digital Humanities Quarterly*, 5(1). Available at: www.digitalhumanities.org /dhq/vol/5/1/000091/000091.html.

(2014). *Graphesis: Visual Forms of Knowledge Production*. Cambridge, MA: Harvard University Press.

(2017). Why distant reading isn't. *PMLA*, 132, 628–35.

Duncan, C. A., Eppstein, D., Goodrich, M. T., Kobourov, S. G., & Nöllenburg, M. (2010). Lombardi drawings of graphs. In U. Brandes & S. Cornelsen, eds., *Graph Drawing 2010: Lecture Notes in Computer Science, vol. 6502*. Berlin: Springer, 195–207.

Düring, M. (2016). How reliable are centrality measures for data collected from fragmentary and heterogeneous historical sources? A case study. In T. Brughmans, A. Collar, & F. S. Coward, eds., *The Connected Past: Challenges to Network Studies in Archaeology and History*. Oxford: Oxford University Press, 85–102.

Edelstein, D., Findlen, P., Ceserani, G., Winterer, C., & Coleman, N. (2017). Historical research in a digital age: Reflections from the Mapping the Republic of Letters Project. *American Historical Review*, 122, 400–24.

Ferguson, N. (2017). *The Square and the Tower: Networks, Hierarchies and the Struggle for Global Power*. London: Penguin UK, Allen Lane Imprint.

Fish, S. (ongoing). *Opinionator* blog. *New York Times*. Available at: https://opinionator.blogs.nytimes.com.

Fogel, R. W. & Engerman, S. L. (1974). *Time on the Cross: The Economics of American Negro Slavery*. London: Little, Brown.

Freeman, L. C. (1977). Set of measures of centrality based on betweenness. *Sociometry*, 40, 35–41.

   (2004). *The Development of Social Network Analysis: A Study in the Sociology of Science*. Vancouver: Empirical Press.

Fry, B. (2007). *Visualizing Data: Exploring and Explaining Data with the Processing Environment*. Sebastopol, CA: O'Reilly Media.

   (2016). Learning from Lombardi. *Medium*. Available at: https://medium.com/@ben_fry/learning-from-lombardi-a28032a7eb5.

Galison, P. (1997). *Image and Logic: A Material Culture of Microphysics*. Chicago: University of Chicago Press.

Gorman, M. E. (2010). *Trading Zones and Interactional Expertise: Creating New Kinds of Collaboration*. Cambridge, MA: MIT Press.

Graham, S., Milligan, I., & Weingart, S. (2015). *Exploring Big Historical Data: The Historian's Macroscope*. London: Imperial College Press.

Graham, S. & Weingart, S. (2015). The equifinality of archaeological networks: An agent-based exploratory lab approach. *Journal of Archaeological Method and Theory*, 22, 248–74.

Grandjean, M. (2015). Social network analysis and visualisation: Moreno's Sociograms revisited. Available at: www.martingrandjean.ch/social-network-analysis-visualization-morenos-sociograms-revisited/.

Goldstone, P. (2015). The artist who obsessed the FBI. *The Daily Beast*, 13 December. Available at: www.thedailybeast.com/the-artist-who-obsessed-the-fbi.

Guare, J. (1990). *Six Degrees of Separation: A Play*. New York: Vintage Books.

Guldi, J. & Armitage, D. (2014). *The History Manifesto*. Cambridge: Cambridge University Press.

Gutman, H. (1975). *Slavery and the Numbers Games*. Urbana: University of Illinois Press.

Healy, K. (2015). The performativity of networks. *European Journal of Sociology*, 56, 175–205.

Hobbs, R. (2003). *Mark Lombardi: Global Networks*. New York: Independent Curators.

Holme, P. (2019). Rare and everywhere: Perspectives on scale-free networks. *Nature Communications*, 10, 1016.

Holme, P., Kim, B. J., Yoon, C. N., & Han, S. K. (2002). Attack vulnerability of complex networks. *Physical Review E*, 65, 056109.

Holme, P. & Saramäki, J. (2013). *Temporal Networks*. Cham: Springer. (2019). *Temporal Network Theory*. Cham: Springer.

Hunt, T. (1846). *Unity of the Iron Network; Showing How the Last Argument for the Break of Gauge, Competition, Is at Variance with the True Interests of the Public*. London: Smith Elder and Company.

Hyvönen, E., Ahnert, R., Ahnert, S. E., Tuominen, J., Mäkelä, F. , Lewis, M. , & Filarski, G. (2019). Reconciling metadata. In H. Hotson & T. Wallnig, eds., *Reassembling the Republic of Letters in the Digital Age: Standards, Systems, Scholarship*. Gottingen: Gottingen University Press, 223–36.

Kapferer, B. (1972). *Strategy and Transaction in an African factory*. Manchester: Manchester University Press.

Karinthy, F. (1929). '*Chain-Links*'. Translated by A. Makkai and edited by E. Jankó. Available at: https://djjr-courses.wdfiles.com/local–files/soc180%3Akarinthy-chain-links/Karinthy-Chain-Links_1929.pdf.

King, J. (2017). Speech to the National Cybersecurity Centre in London. Available at: https://ec.europa.eu/commission/commissioners/2014–2019/king/announcements/commissioner-king's-speech-national-cybersecurity-centrelondon_en.

Klein, L. (2018). Distant reading after Moretti. Available at: http://lklein.com/2018/01/distant-reading-after-moretti/.

Krebs, V. E. (2001). Mapping networks of terrorist cells. *Connections*, 24(3), 43–52.

Kruja, E., Marks, J., Blair, A., & Waters, R. (2002). A short note on the history of graph drawing. In P. Mutzel, M. Jünger, & S. Leipert, eds.,

Graph Drawing: 9th International Symposium, GD 2001 Vienna, Austria, September 23–26, 2001. Berlin: Springer, 272–86.

Lakoff, G. & Johnson, M. (1980). *Metaphors We Live By*. Chicago: Chicago University Press.

Lakoff, G. & Núñez, R. E. (2000). *Where Mathematics Comes From: How the Embodied Mind Brings Mathematics into Being*. New York: Basic Books.

Larrington, C. (2008).Review of *Constructing Nations, Reconstructing Myth: Essays in Honour of T. A. Shippey*. *Modern Language Review*, 103, 1087–8.

Laterza, V. (2018). Cambridge Analytica, independent research and the national interest. *Anthropology Today*, 34, 1–2.

Latour, B. (1993). *The Pasteurisation of France*. Translated by Alan Sheridan. *Cambridge, MA*: *Harvard University Press*.

   (2005). *Reassembling the Social: An Introduction to Actor-Network-Theory*. Oxford: Oxford University Press.

Lima, M. (2011). Visual complexity. Available at: www.visualcomplexity.com.

Lombardi, M. (2001), The 'Offshore' phenomenon: Dirty banking in a brave new world. *Cabinet*, 2. Available at: www.cabinetmagazine.org/issues/2/dirtybanking.php.

MacCarron, P. & Kenna. R. (2012). Universal properties of mythological networks. *EPL*, 99, 28002.

McLean, C. & Hassard J. (2004). Symmetrical absence/symmetrical absurdity: Critical notes on the production of actor-network accounts. *Journal of Management Studies*, 41(3),493–519.

Meirelles, I. (2018). Visualizing information. In J. Flanders & F. Jannidis, eds., *The Shape of Data in the Digital Humanities: Modeling Texts and Text-Based Resources*. Abingdon: Routledge, 167–77.

Michel, J.-B., Shen, Y. K., & Aiden, A. P., Veres, A. , Gray, M. K., The Google Books Team, Pickett, J. P., Hoiberg, D., Clancy, D., Norvig, P., Orwant, J. Pinker, S., Nowak, M. A., & Erez

Lieberman, A. (2011). Quantitative analysis of culture using millions of digitised books. *Science*, 331, 176–82.

Milgram, S. (1967). The small world problem. *Psychology Today*, 2, 60–7.

Mol, A. (2010) Actor-network theory: Sensitive terms and enduring tensions. *Kölner Zeitschrift für Soziologie und Sozialpsychologie*, 50, 253–69.

Moreno J. [& Jennings, H. H.] (1953). *Who Shall Survive? Foundations of Sociometry, Group Psychotherapy and Sociodrama*. 2nd ed. New York: Beacon House.

Moretti, F. (2011). Network theory, plot analysis. *Literary Lab Pamphlet 2*. https://litlab.stanford.edu/LiteraryLabPamphlet2.pdf

Otlet, P. (1918). Transformations operées dans l'appareil bibliographique des sciences. *Revue Scientifique*, 58, 236–41.

Pechenick, E. A., Danforth, C. M., & Dodds, P. S. (2015). Characterizing the Google Books corpus: Strong limits to inferences of socio-cultural and linguistic evolution. *PLoS ONE*, e0137041.

Pinski, G. & Narin, F. (1976). Citation influence for journal aggregates of scientific publications: Theory, with application to the literature of physics. *Information Processing & Management*, 12, 297–312.

Pitts, F. R. (1965). A graph-theoretic approach to historical geography. *Professional Geographer*, 17, 15–20.

Price, D. J. de Solla (1965). Networks of scientific papers: The pattern of bibliometric references indicates the nature of the scientific research front. *Science*, 149, 510–15.

Radden, G. (2002). How metonymic are metaphors? In A. Barcelona, ed., *Metaphor and Metonymy at the Crossroads: A Cognitive Perspective*. Berlin: Mouton de Gruyter, 93–108.

Rawson, K. & Muñoz, T. (2019). Against cleaning. In M. K. Gold & L. F. Klein, eds., *DH Debates 2019*. Minneapolis: University of Minnesota Press. Available at: https://dhdebates.gc.cuny.edu/projects/debates-in-the-digital-humanities-2019.

Ray, D. & Robson, A. (2018). Certified random: A new order for coauthorship. *American Economic Review*, 108, 489–520.

Rendgen, S. & Weidemann, J. (2012). *Information Graphics*. Cologne: Taschen.

Rosenberg, D. (2013). Data before the fact. In L. Gitelman, ed., *'Raw Data' Is an Oxymoron*. Cambridge, MA: MIT Press, 15–40.

   (2016). Against infographics. *Art Journal*, 75. Available at: http://artjour nal.collegeart.org/?p=6993.

Ryan, Y. C. (2018). More difficult from Dublin than from Dieppe. *Media History*, 24, 458–76.

Saaty, T. (1977). A scaling method for priorities in hierarchical structures. *Journal of Mathematical Psychology*, 15, 234–81.

Schich, M., Song, C., Ahn, Y.-Y., Mirsky, A. , Martino, M. , Barabási, A.-L., & Helbing, D. (2014). A network framework of cultural history. *Science*, 345, 558–62.

Smiraglia, R. P. & Van den Heuvel, C. (2011). Idea collider: From a theory of knowledge organisation to a theory of knowledge interaction. *Bulletin of the American Society for Information Science and Technology*, 37(4), 43–7.

Snow, C. P. (1998). *The Two Cultures*. With an introduction by Stefan Collini. Cambridge: Cambridge University Press.

So, R. J. & Long, H. (2013). Network analysis and the sociology of modernism. *boundary 2*, 40, 147–82.

Squire, M. & Elsner, J. (2016). Sight and memory: The visual art of Roman mnemonics. In M. Squire, ed., *Sight and the Ancient Senses*. Abingdon: Routledge, 180–204.

Svensson, P. (2012). Beyond the big tent. In M. K. Gold, ed., *Debates in the Digital Humanities*. Minneapolis: University of Minnesota Press, 36–49.

Terras, M. & Nyhan, J. (2016). Father Busa's female punch card operatives. In M. K. Gold & L. F. Klein, eds., *Debates in the Digital Humanities 2016*. Minneapolis: University of Minnesota Press, 60–5.

Trompf, G. W. (2011). The classification of the sciences and the quest for interdisciplinarity: A brief history of ideas from ancient philosophy to contemporary environmental science. *Environmental Conservation*, 38, 113–26.

Tukey, J. W. (1977). *Exploratory Data Analysis*. Reading, PA: Addison-Wesley.

Tversky, B. (2014). Visualizing thought. In *Handbook of Human Centric Visualization*. New York: Springer, 3–40.

Tversky, B., & Suwa, M. (2009). Thinking with sketches. In *Tools for Innovation*. Oxford: Oxford University Press.

Uboldi, G., Caviglia, G., Coleman, N., Heymann, S. , Mantegari, G. , & Ciuccarelli, P. (2013). Knot: An interface for the study of social networks in the humanities. In F. Garzotto, M. Zancanaro, A. De Angeli, & F. Paternò, eds., *Proceedings of the Biannual Conference of the Italian Chapter of SIGCHI: 2013, Trento, Italy : CHItaly '13*, article 15.

Underwood, T. (2019a). Dear humanists: Fear not the digital revolution. *The Chronicle of Higher Education*, 27 March. Available at: www.chronicle.com/article/Dear-Humanists-Fear-Not-the/245987.

(2019b). *Distant Horizons: Digital Evidence and Literary Change*. Chicago: University of Chicago Press.

Van den Heuvel, C. (2012). Multidimensional classifications: Past and future conceptualisations and visualisations. *Knowledge Organisation*, 39, 446–60.

Venturini, T., Jacomy, M., & Jensen, P. (2019). What do we see when we look at networks/ An introduction to visual network analysis and force-directed layouts. Available at: https://ssrn.com/abstract=3378438.

Vosoughi, S., Roy, D., & Aral, S. (2018). The spread of true and false news online. *Science* 359, 1146–51.

Watts, D. J. (2004). *Six Degrees: The Science of a Connected Age*. London: Vintage.

Watts, D. J. & Strogatz, S. H. (1998). Collective dynamics of 'small-world' networks. *Nature*, 393, 440–2.

Weingart, S. (under review). *The Networked Structure of Early Modern Science*, Manuscript.

   (2012). Networks demystified 3: The power law rant. Available at: http://scottbot.net/networks-demystified-3-the-power-law-rant/.

   (2013). Networks demystified 8: When networks are inappropriate. Available at: http://scottbot.net/networks-demystified-8-when-networks-are-inappropriate/.

   (2014a). The moral role of DH in a data-driven world. Available at: https://scottbot.net/networked-society/.

   (2014b). Bridging token and type. Available at: https://scottbot.net/bridging-token-and-type/.

Witmore, M. (2016). Latour, the digital humanities, and the divided kingdom of knowledge. *New Literary History*, 47, 353–75.

Yeo, R. (1991). Reading encyclopedias: Science and the organisation of knowledge in British dictionaries of arts and sciences, 1730–1850. *Isis*, 82, 24–49.

Zachary, W. W. (1977). An information flow model for conflict and fission in small groups. *Journal of Anthropological Research*, 33, 452–73.

Acknowledgements

This Element began as a series of conversations (often over cocktails) between Nicole, Ruth, and Sebastian when the latter pair were visiting fellows at Stanford University in 2015–16. During that year, Ruth was invited to co-organise the annual Text Technologies Collegium with Elaine Treharne on the topic of networks. Scott was one of the participants at this event, and thereafter the four of us set about writing a short pamphlet or manifesto, which eventually evolved into this Element.

The arguments we make in these pages have been shaped by ongoing exchange with a whole network of colleagues and friends, who have shared and debated ideas and advised, mentored, and challenged us. We are hugely thankful to Jo Guldi and to our Elements 'gathering' editor, Laura Dietz, who both read and commented on the manuscript in full. The two anonymous readers provided shrewd advice that we have sought to heed. Any remaining faults and infelicities are, of course, our own. We are all grateful for the communities that grew up around the Arts Humanities and Complex Networks satellite workshops to NetSci, organised by Max Schich, Isabel Meirelles, and Roger Malina; to the rotating cast that came through the Early Modern Digital Agenda Institutes at the Folger Shakespeare Library, directed by Owen Williams and Jonathan Hope; to the extensive network assembled by Howard Hotson and Thomas Wallnig for the COST Action Reassembling the Republic of Letters; and for the excellent groups of people assembled for the Getty Institute Network Analysis and Digital Art History, the Dagstuhl Seminar for Network Visualization in the Humanities, and the IPAM/NEH summer institute for Networks and Network Analysis for the Humanities. We would also like to express our combined thanks to Mark Algee-Hewitt, Dan Edelstein, Marten Düring, Charles van den Heuvel, John Ladd, Matthew Lincoln, Laura Mandell, Sarah Ogilvie, Daniel Shore, Tim Tangherlini, Elaine Treharne, and Chris Warren for productive discussions that have extended and enriched our thinking.

In addition, Ruth and Sebastian would like to acknowledge the influence of their ongoing collaborations on early modern letter networks with Howard Hotson, Arno Bosse, Miranda Lewis, Esther van Raamsdonk, Yann Ryan, and Philip Beeley. They are both grateful to Mary Flannery for helping organise the writing retreat in Neuchâtel that kick-started the writing of this book. Ruth would like to thank the AHRC and Stanford Humanities Center, who funded work that started some of the thinking found in these pages. Markman Ellis, Howard Hotson, the late Lisa Jardine, and Daniel Wakelin wrote letters in support of those fellowship applications, and she is immensely thankful for their belief in her various projects. She is also grateful to the School of English and Drama at Queen Mary University of London, who supported her through the network turn in her career, especially Warren Boutcher, Andrea Brady, Jerry Brotton, David Colclough, Rachael Gilmour, and Joad Raymond. Sebastian would like to thank CESTA at Stanford for welcoming him and for providing a space to work and collaborate. He would also like to thank the Royal Society and the Gatsby Foundation for their financial support during the writing of this book.

The Stanford Humanities Center, the Stanford Libraries, and CESTA provided fertile environments for research that were essential to Nicole's contribution to this project. She is particularly grateful to all of the researchers who have been a part of Humanities + Design at CESTA (including her co-authors) where many of the ideas expressed in this book were tested, debated, and enacted, beginning with the Early Modern Time & Networks Research Workshop. Humanities + Design would not have been possible without Dan Edelstein's spirit, energy, and wisdom, Giovanna Ceserani's generosity, commitment, and attention to detail, Giorgio Caviglia's talent for nurturing and giving elegant form to our ideas, or Ethan Jewett's tireless and creative engineering efforts. Nicole would also like to thank the Office of Digital Humanities at the National Endowment for the Humanities and the Andrew W. Mellon Foundation for supporting the work of Humanities + Design over the years.

Scott would additionally like to thank Bob Hatch, Katy Börner, and Cassidy Sugimoto for their continued guidance and support, and Jessica

Otis, Matt Lavin, Matt Burton, Shawn Graham, Ian Milligan, Micki Kaufmann, and Zoe LeBlanc for the countless thoughtful discussions on networks and the humanities. He is especially grateful to Laurie Taylor and her family. Without the writing retreat spent in their beautiful, temporarily vacant home, he surely would not have finished his portion of the book. Finally, thanks must go to Nechama Weingart, without whom Scott could not see the forest for the trees.

Cambridge Elements ⹀

Publishing and Book Culture

SERIES EDITOR

Samantha Rayner
University College London

Samantha Rayner is a Reader in UCL's Department of
Information Studies. She is also Director of UCL's Centre for
Publishing, co-Director of the Bloomsbury CHAPTER
(Communication History, Authorship, Publishing, Textual
Editing and Reading) and co-Editor of the Academic Book of
the Future BOOC (Book as Open Online Content) with UCL
Press.

ASSOCIATE EDITOR

Leah Tether
University of Bristol

Leah Tether is Professor of Medieval Literature and Publishing
at the University of Bristol. With an academic background in
medieval French and English literature and a professional
background in trade publishing, Leah has combined her
expertise and developed an international research profile in
book and publishing history from manuscript to digital.

About the Series

This series aims to fill the demand for easily accessible, quality texts available for teaching and research in the diverse and dynamic fields of Publishing and Book Culture. Rigorously researched and peer-reviewed Elements will be published under themes, or 'Gatherings'. These Elements should be the first check point for researchers or students working on that area of publishing and book trade history and practice: we hope that, situated so logically at Cambridge University Press, where academic publishing in the UK began, it will develop to create an unrivalled space where these histories and practices can be investigated and preserved.

Cambridge Elements ☰

Publishing and Book Culture
Digital Literary Culture

Gathering Editor: Laura Dietz
Laura Dietz is a Senior Lecturer in Writing and Publishing in
the Cambridge School of Creative Industries at Anglia Ruskin
University. She writes novels and studies novels, publishing
fiction alongside research on topics such as e-novel readership,
the digital short story, online literary magazines, and the
changing definition of authorship in the digital era.

ELEMENTS IN THE GATHERING

The Network Turn: Changing Perspectives in the Humanities
Ruth Ahnert, Sebastian E. Ahnert, Catherine Nicole Coleman and Scott
B. Weingart

A full series listing is available at: www.cambrige.org/EPBC

Printed in the United States
by Baker & Taylor Publisher Services